m

mettle

BIBLE READING NOTES

TO INSPIRE COURAGE SPIRIT CHARACTER

MIX
Paper from
responsible sources
FSC® C015900

CONTENTS

WELCOME TO
mettle
COURAGE SPIRIT CHARACTER ...

LET'S KICK OFF this issue with some core material on the idea of discipleship. The twelve guys who hung around with Jesus are generally known as 'The Disciples'. So can we be disciples of Jesus too? And if so, what does that mean for how we think, speak and act?

In our Hot Potatoes we'll look first at the effect of peer pressure. How can we withstand pressure from others and choose to do what is right? Next we look at humour – a beautiful thing if used well. Even Jesus used humour to communicate truth. What is humour good for and how can we use it to build up others? Last, we unpack the idea of obedience. Who should we obey, how and when?

Get stuck in!

The *Mettle* Team

READ:
1 CORINTHIANS 2:10–16

KEY VERSE
V16

'But we have the mind of Christ.'

PT1
DISCIPLESHIP

WELCOME TO THE first topic of this issue of *Mettle* – discipleship.

What is the way ahead? Do you know who to follow? Do you know why you should follow? How do you decide?

A famous scientist had a very good model of the solar system on her desk. Completely to scale, it showed all the planets circling the sun. A friend, who didn't believe in God, saw it and asked the scientist who had made it, because he wanted to get one. The scientist saw an opportunity and asked her friend, 'What do you mean:

"Who made it?" What a silly question! Nobody made it, it just appeared.' Her friend was not impressed: 'Just tell me who made it! Things like that don't just appear! Someone must have made it.' The scientist looked at her friend and smiled: 'You're right, somebody did make it. But here's the thing: you refuse to believe that this model just happened without a maker, so why do you believe that the real universe could exist without a creator?'

Do you know what you believe as a Christian – and why? Jesus encouraged people to ask questions so that they could discover more about God. Be confident that God created you for a reason and that Jesus wants you to follow His example. Over the next two weeks we will be focusing on six key characteristics, learning some top discipleship tips and looking at what it means to be one of Jesus' disciples in today's world.

↑ **PRAY**

Father, thank You for creating the universe and for making me. Help me to understand more about You and to be willing to take opportunities to talk to others about You. Amen.

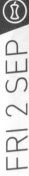

FRI 2 SEP

READ:
PROVERBS 3:4-6

KEY VERSE v5
'Trust in the LORD with all your heart and lean not on your own understanding'

THE DICTIONARY DEFINES a disciple as somebody who believes in and follows the teachings of a leader, a philosophy or a religion.

Hidden within this word search are six words that describe a disciple. Over the next few days we'll be unpacking them together. The word for today is **Believer**. Hebrews 13:8 tells us, 'Jesus Christ is the same yesterday and today and for ever.'

A	S	D	R	F	G	B	M
C	U	H	L	I	R	E	L
U	P	P	U	P	I	L	I
Z	P	Q	J	M	D	I	Y
F	O	L	L	O	W	E	R
P	R	S	W	B	Q	V	X
K	T	U	H	V	C	E	D
L	E	A	R	N	E	R	W
E	R	A	L	O	H	C	S

Have you ever stopped and asked yourself what you believe, what you trust in? Today's reading encourages us to trust in the Lord and to turn to Him for advice (v6).

DISCIPLESHIP TIP 1:
Believe and trust in Jesus with all your heart.

THINK
Who do you turn to for advice? Do you ever take it? Are you confident in trusting Jesus? Peter, one of Jesus' first disciples, was so confident that he got out of a boat and walked on water (Matt. 14:28–29). Are you willing to believe what Jesus has said and put it into practice?

WEEKEND
3/4 SEP

READ:
ROMANS 12:1–8

KEY VERSE V1

'offer your bodies as a living sacrifice, holy and pleasing to God'

THE WORD FOR today is **Follower**. For you to be a disciple of Jesus you need to give yourself to God. As we grow in our love for Him, everything we have can be offered to Him – our money, our time, our family, our home, our job, our thoughts, our moods, our love, our ambitions and even our iPhone!

To be honest this is really hard to understand and I sometimes struggle with the idea that, as a follower of Christ, I could be asked to offer everything I have, including my family, as a sacrifice to God. But I am comforted by the fact that He has never before asked for more than

CONTINUED►►

- He knew I was able to give at the time. As verse 2 says: 'let God transform you into a new person by changing the way you think. Then you will learn to know God's will for you, which is good and pleasing and perfect.' (NLT)

DISCIPLESHIP TIP 2:
Be willing to offer your all to God so that you can become all He has in store for you.

THINK
What does 'your all' actually mean? Re-read the list in the first paragraph of today's notes and write down everything that is important to you. Be honest and list the things you'd struggle to offer to God. Then pray. Ask for God's help to let these things go if, and when, He needs you to.

KEY VERSE v27

'Where, then, is boasting? It is excluded. Because of what law? The law that requires works? No, because of the "law" that requires faith.'

THE WORD FOR today is **Learner**. A disciple is someone who learns from their rabbi (a Jewish word that Jesus and the disciples would have used) or teacher. To be specific, in order to be a disciple of Christ we need to learn about Him and from Him. Knowing Jesus enables us to know the way to God. To know Jesus we have to learn to have faith in His teaching, in the Bible and in the experience of the Holy Spirit.

To put it simply, if we truly want to know God, it doesn't matter how good we are, how much money we give to charity, whether we work on Sundays, or attend all the church services we can. It is only through our faith in Jesus and what He has done for us that we are accepted by God.

None of us can boast that we are better in God's sight than anyone else. We are all the same; loved and cared for by God.

DISCIPLESHIP TIP 3:
Have faith in Jesus and learn all we can about Him.

PRAY
Father, help me to grow in my faith. Teach me more about Jesus, and let me experience that confidence as I talk to others. I want to learn more about You and the amazing love You have for me. Amen.

READ:
HEBREWS 11:1-13

KEY VERSE V 1

'faith is confidence in what we hope for and assurance about what we do not see.'

THE WORD TODAY is **Pupil**. Top athletes have coaches for every aspect of their game – even though they are already great at their sport, they will spend hours training; learning from their coaches and perfecting their skills. A star athlete constantly learns and strives to perform better.

Yesterday we looked at the importance of learning to have faith. But what is faith? It is the 'confidence in what we hope for and assurance about what we do not see' (Heb. 11:1, NLT).

Today's verses go on to give examples of biblical characters who show great faith. Noah builds an enormous boat on land to save the animals and his family. Abraham leaves home to follow God's instructions, although he doesn't know where he will end up.

Are you still willing to be taught by others? The heroes in Hebrews didn't need to see the short-term end, they were focusing on the long term – an eternity spent with God.

DISCIPLESHIP TIP 4:
Be willing to be taught by others. Think about the idea of being mentored. Do you know someone older/wiser/more experienced than you, who you respect and could mentor you?

PRAY
Father, thank You for the faithful example set by others; may I also be an example to others. I pray that I will grow in the confidence that You have good plans for me, even if I can't see how those plans will come about right now. Amen.

KEY VERSE V2

'you granted him authority over all people'

THE WORD FOR today is **Scholar**. Jesus had power and authority and He used them! He gave the blind their sight, He healed people who couldn't walk and He saw straight into the hearts of people, helping them to sort out their lives. Everyone who came into contact with Jesus experienced God. Some didn't like that experience and ran from it.

But what does this mean to us today? Jesus gives eternal life, as the Samaritan woman at the well experienced (John 4). He knew what she really needed and offered her water that would quench her thirst forever. Because Jesus has this all-encompassing authority, He has the ability to offer us exactly what we need. He isn't some bearded, long-haired, sandal-wearing guy in a picture – He is the Son of God! He is powerful! He is awesome!

DISCIPLESHIP TIP 5:

Study the Bible, get to know God's teaching and become a scholar who knows God deeply – not just enough to get by.

Over the next few days we'll look at Jesus' prayer in John 17. It highlights what Jesus wanted His Father to give to His disciples. ▲

 CHALLENGE

Ask God to talk to you about your needs and how to meet them. Find somewhere quiet or go for a walk to allow yourself space to listen to His response. Set apart time to follow this up. You could join a Bible study group – or even start one yourself.

READ:
JOHN 17:3-4

KEY VERSE V3

'this is eternal life: that they know you, the only true God, and Jesus Christ, whom you have sent.'

THE WORD FOR today is **Supporter**. How do we get the eternal life mentioned in today's reading? By knowing Jesus and understanding that it was God who sent Him to earth.

I like Disney-Pixar films. In *Finding Nemo*, Crush the turtle is having a conversation with Marlin about trusting and letting go. Marlin asks him: 'But when do you know?' and the response is: 'You know when you know, you know.' At which point they both nod knowingly, but then a confused look crosses Marlin's face.

When do we know 'the only true God, and Jesus'? It's the same answer: 'You know when you know, you know.' You can have all the facts laid out, but when you're filled with the Holy Spirit, you experience a new dimension of knowing God. Being a supporter means getting to know who you support better and better, which engages your emotions as well as your mind.

DISCIPLESHIP TIP 6:
Being a supporter also usually means that you tell people about who you support and why. Tell others about God, and understand that it is His Holy Spirit who reveals who He is to them.

PRAY
Father, I want to know You more and to know Your presence in my life. Help me to recognise You and to tell others about You every day. Amen.

KEY VERSE V7

'Now they know that everything you have given me comes from you.'

WHAT DOES IT mean to be a disciple? For Jesus' disciples, it meant incredible experiences, but it also meant being challenged on what they believed.

Jesus and His disciples spent three years together, travelling, teaching and testifying. The disciples saw Jesus do amazing things: from feeding the five thousand to sharing eternal water with the woman at the well; from walking on water to calming a storm; from healing the Roman officer's servant to bringing Lazarus back to life.

Yet it was only in the last few months together that Jesus actually challenged them to say who they believed Him to be (Matt. 16:15–16). And, only in the last few days did Jesus draw together all of what the disciples had seen and heard. As we follow Jesus, it's helpful to look back on what He's done for us and what it means. In doing so we get fresh insights into who Jesus really is.

DISCIPLESHIP TIP 7:
Make time to think about what you have learnt about God. Try keeping a journal to jot down anything you find really interesting or helpful.

THINK
Like in a thriller movie, all the pieces don't fall into place until the last minute. Jesus was confirming to God that His disciples knew Him; knew He had come from God and now knew that everything He had done was through God.

READ:
GENESIS 3:1–7

KEY VERSE
V6

'she took some and ate it. She also gave some to her husband, who was with her, and he ate it.'

PEER PRESSURE PT1

OVER THE NEXT couple of weeks we're going to be thinking about peer pressure – what it is, how it can occur, how it influences us and what it can make us do. Then later on, in Part Two, we take a look at how we can cope with the peer pressure around us.

So when did it all start? Well, the first instance of peer pressure comes pretty quickly after creation. Eve takes a bite from the forbidden fruit, and then passes it on to Adam – now what should he do?

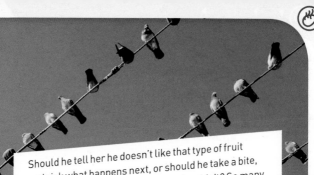

Should he tell her he doesn't like that type of fruit and risk what happens next, or should he take a bite, even though he knows full well he shouldn't? So many factors to take into account, so many reasons to go one way or the other – all over a very simple question: does he eat the fruit or not?

Each of us will face situations like this on a regular basis. They probably won't centre on fruit produce, but they will involve us having to make a choice. We have to think about what it is that's going to motivate our decisions: are we going to decide what to do based on what people around us do, say and think? Or are we going to base our choices on something else, something deeper? No one is saying that this is an easy question, but it's one we'll face throughout our lives.

THINK

As we start looking at the issue of peer pressure, spend a few moments in quiet, being honest with God. When do you succumb to peer pressure? What are the situations that force you to make the choice between leading and being led by others? Think about how you view peer pressure.

KEY VERSE v70

'But he denied it before them all. "I don't know what you're talking about," he said.'

I'VE ALWAYS FELT a bit sorry for Peter. He was probably a decent guy who had done a pretty good job of following Jesus and doing everything he'd been taught. This was probably his one and only major mistake, and yet it's laid bare for all to read about. We know he makes up for it later on, but still – I'm not sure I'd like my failures recorded so publicly.

Peter is faced with a problem: he knows he should remain faithful to Jesus, just as he promised he would, but he's really worried what might happen if he's seen to be 'one of them'. Eventually the pressure is just too much – and he gives in. Peter gets quite angry as he lies to the people around him, maintaining that he is not a follower of Jesus.

I'm sure that some of us would say we'd stand up for what we believed in, but how true would that be? What would it take to make us fold; to give up and pretend to be something we're not? How often in school or out with our mates are we scared about what might happen if we tell the truth? Peter's declaration reminds us that it takes real courage in the face of extreme peer pressure to stand up for what we believe in. Could we withstand the pressure? What would it take to make us fold?

PRAY

Spend a few moments asking God to forgive you for the times when peer pressure has made you scared and you've not been faithful to what you believe.

TUES 13 SEP

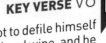

'But Daniel resolved not to defile himself with the royal food and wine, and he asked the chief official for permission not to defile himself in this way.'

EVERY COMMUNITY HAS certain customs and rituals of its own. Whether it's our class at school, our football team or our drama group, the group will do things because that's the way they've 'always done them'. These customs or traditions are passed on from old to new members, and are often taken for granted. But sometimes there comes a moment when we have to stop and think: is what they've always done right – and is it right for me?

Daniel and his friends, prisoners in a foreign land, found themselves having to learn a new language and a new culture. Part of the culture involved partaking of the same food and drink as the others working at the palace. However, Daniel and his friends wanted to obey God's laws about clean and unclean food, which meant limiting themselves to fruit and veg (their 5-a-day) rather than eating what was being offered.

Despite the pressure to conform, he battled against custom and proved that God's way was better. How often do we just do what we've always done rather than doing something new, something better? Tradition can be a good thing, but it's sometimes just the pressure of long-dead peers to keep things as they've always been.

PRAY
Dear God, help me to do what is right and to follow Your way. Give me strength to continue to live for You. Amen.

READ:
MARK 15:6-15

KEY VERSE V11

'But the chief priests stirred up the crowd to get Pilate to release Barabbas instead.'

'WHY DID YOU do that?' asked the teacher. 'Everyone else was doing it, sir,' replied the pupil. I wonder how many times a conversation similar to this takes place in schools up and down the country. Group mentality can be a dangerous thing – people in a crowd do and say things they would never dream of doing of their own volition.

Today's passage is a chilling reminder of what can happen when peer pressure takes over a crowd. As individuals, if asked, I guess most of those there in front of Pontius Pilate would have given the 'Get out of jail free' card to Jesus rather than to a convicted criminal and murderer. As it was, a little pressure from the local religious leaders and all of a sudden the crowd were baying for Jesus' blood. We don't know whether the chief priests threatened, bribed or reasoned with those present, but the pressure they exerted was obvious.

Are you someone who goes along with the crowd? Do you get caught up in the group mentality and find that you're doing or saying things because everyone else is? Being the one who says no in a crowd of people saying yes can be terrifying, but at least you'll know that you weren't part of a group making the wrong choice.

PRAY

Lord, give me the boldness to do what is right, and Your protection when I find I need to go against what everyone else is doing. Amen.

READ:
EXODUS 32:1–6

KEY VERSE V1

'When the people saw that Moses was so long in coming down from the mountain, they gathered round Aaron'

THE ISRAELITES WERE tired, hungry, thirsty and fed up. They'd left Egypt ready for something new, something better. What they'd got was desert and more desert. Now their leader had left them and wandered off up a mountain. All in all, I imagine they were getting a bit irritated with the whole thing.

Meanwhile, Moses' brother, Aaron, was faced with dealing with an increasingly disaffected people who wanted immediate guidance. They didn't know when Moses was due back, so they decided to try to get the direction they wanted from idols made of gold. Aaron must have known this wasn't the best of plans, but he also knew that objecting to their idea wouldn't go down well. So he agreed, and the Israelites ended up in a whole new heap of trouble.

You might ask why Aaron didn't just tell the Israelites to be patient and wait until Moses returned. Peer pressure can sometimes appear very threatening. We don't want to let down the people around us, nor to find out what will happen if we do, so we end up doing things we'd never have dreamed of. However, remember that whatever our decision, we're going to have to live with the consequences.

THINK
Do I put pressure on the people around me? How can I change this?

19

READ:
DANIEL 3:1–30

 KEY VERSE V7

'as they heard the sound ... all the nations and peoples of every language fell down and worshipped the image of gold'

A FEW YEARS ago, the government ran an odd advert to try and discourage young people from smoking. It showed some teenagers doing all the things teen smokers do, but rather than having cigarettes, they had party noisemakers.

The sight of these teenagers rushing into the toilets to have a quick blow on these kazoo-like toys came across as pretty odd, highlighting the fact that smoking is, in reality, a really stupid thing to do! Now, many of you may be sitting there proudly saying to yourselves: 'Aha! I don't smoke. It doesn't interest me.' But how often do we do something just as silly – just because the people around us are doing it?

There's something about the effects of peer pressure that seems to rob otherwise intelligent people of their common sense. People will wear completely off-the-wall combinations of clothes, just because everyone's wearing them. They'll buy particular things, or listen to particular music, just because it's the fashion – regardless of the logic behind their choices. Sometimes it takes a cold, hard look in the mirror to see the things we do just because other people do them. What do you do just because ...?

THINK
Spend some time reflecting on how peer pressure leads you to do things you'd never contemplate normally. Ask God to help you stop doing these things.

WEEKEND
17/18 SEP

READ:
1 JOHN 2:15–17

KEY VERSE v16

'For everything in the world – the lust of the flesh, the lust of the eyes, and the pride of life – comes not from the Father but from the world.'

WHILE WATCHING TELEVISION, I noticed that advert after advert showed me things I might want. Another games console, an amazing phone, the latest clothing lines, an exciting new movie – the list of desirable objects went on and on and on. There is a tremendous pressure to own the latest phone or possess this season's most popular trainers.

This pressure is increased when it's not just the television prodding us to own these things but also the people around us. We see what others have – and we want it. Our friend is the first in the class to own the latest iPhone, and we see

CONTINUED▶

▼ how cool it makes him look, so we want it too.
Everyone else seems to have a particular make of
▼ shoes – so we just have to have them as well!

Today's Bible verses sum it up quite nicely – the
▼ world offers us a craving for physical pleasure
▼ and for the things we see around us. However, we
are called to crave something very different. God
wants us to seek the things of His kingdom rather
▼ than the things which adorn the material world.

▼ We are called to withstand the constant
pressure from the media and from our peers to
buy, buy, buy, and are asked to think about what it
▼ is we give, give, give. How do we contribute to the
▼ world around us? How do we make our schools
and communities a little bit more how Jesus
would want them?

➲ CHALLENGE

**How often do you look at the things your friends
have – and covet them? What are you thinking of
buying that you could possibly live without? Are
you being pressured into buying something you
don't need?**

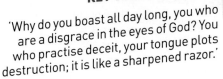

KEY VERSES vv 1-2

'Why do you boast all day long, you who
are a disgrace in the eyes of God? You
who practise deceit, your tongue plots
destruction; it is like a sharpened razor.'

MON 19 SEP

HOW MANY OF us would consider ourselves expert liars? They
say practice makes perfect and, if we're brave enough to admit
it, some of us will have had a lot of practice at lying to those
around us. Most of them are probably small lies – ones we
don't really notice, but they're still part of the problem.

The trouble is, it can often be much easier to lie than to
tell the truth. There can often be huge pressure on us to
say we've done certain things, or that we watch certain TV
programmes, and the easiest way to save face in these
situations is just to lie about it. 'Did you see so-and-so
programme last night?' 'Ah, yeah, it was great.'

We know that all the cool kids watched it and, even though
we might not have wanted to watch that programme, it's
easier to lie to our friends to save face, rather than admit
the truth about what we like and dislike. The trouble is: little
lies lead to bigger lies, and more dangerous lies, and before
long we're caught up in a situation where we've told so many
lies we can't remember which ones we've told. Surely no
matter what the pressure is, it's better in the long run just to
tell the truth.

CHALLENGE
Count how many lies you tell during the course of just one
day. Be honest and you might be surprised!

READ:
1 CORINTHIANS 6:12–20

KEY VERSE V18

'Flee from sexual immorality. All other sins a person commits are outside the body, but whoever sins sexually, sins against their own body.'

IT'S USED TO sell chocolate, to add cheap laughs to sitcoms, sell make-up and to convince us that we really need the latest perfume or Lynx deodorant – whether we like it or not, we're surrounded by sex. And with that comes a huge pressure to be having it!

The later you get in your teen years, the more people seem to be doing it, and the odder you feel if you're not. For many, having sex isn't a big deal – it's something teenagers do, and you may feel weird or get teased by others if you're not having sex. However, the Bible paints a very, very different picture.

Today's Bible verse is very straightforward: sexual immorality (sleeping with someone who is not your wife or husband) is not good. It's not how God designed sex to be. But with hormones raging, and your reputation at stake, will you remain part of the very select group of teenagers who choose to save it for their wedding night? With God's help, we can withstand the pressure and the Holy Spirit is able to help us resist the temptations that surround us (Heb. 2:18; 4:15–16; 1 Cor. 10:13). We can also help ourselves by not putting ourselves into situations where we can be tempted, like staying over in our girl/boyfriend's room.

PRAY
God, thank You that You created us to be sexual beings. Help me withstand the pressure to have sex before You intended. Keep me strong in resisting temptation. Amen.

 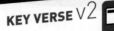
TODAY'S VERSE IN full is quite a mouthful! There's an awful lot contained in a fairly short sentence, but it leaves us with quite a terrifying challenge. It introduces the idea that peer pressure might not always be a bad thing.

There might be times when it's your job to use your influence on the people around you. In the same way that we know we don't always get it right ourselves, there are times when those around us would really benefit from a careful prod in the right direction.

Today's verse tells us that we are called to correct, rebuke and encourage. We are told that we should point out what's not right, show others how it can be made right, and encourage them to get it right. And all this should be done with 'great patience and careful instruction' (v2).

You might know what it's like to teach someone to do something, and you'll have felt the great frustration that comes when people don't get it right first time. It's not hard to prod them back in the right direction (or tell them where they went wrong); the hard bit is to do it in love, with patience.

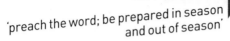

THINK

How are you going to use peer pressure positively to correct, rebuke and encourage, all the time showing great patience? It's certainly something which will require some thinking about, and probably several attempts to get it right!

READ:
HEBREWS 10:19–25

KEY VERSE V24

'And let us consider how we may spur one another on towards love and good deeds'

WHAT KEEPS YOU going? I don't know about you, but sometimes getting out of bed in the morning can be a real struggle – the bed is warm and the world is cold. This results in a real struggle to conquer the sleepiness and start the day.

However, not every day is a struggle. On the days when we know we have something to look forward to, we're out of bed like a shot!

Sometimes life can be a bit like this – doing the right thing can be a real struggle. Peer pressure can be relentless, and withstanding its influence can leave you unpopular – and sometimes unhappy! What you need is some motivation.

Today's verse exhorts its readers to be original in finding ways of motivating others to do what God wants. Each of us needs encouragement to give us the strength to carry on. If we encourage other people, they will encourage us, and we'll find that the journey is just a little bit easier. It might not make it any easier to get out of bed in the morning, but it might make the task of standing up against peer pressure a little more bearable.

 CHALLENGE

How can you use your influence to motivate others to love and good works? Who are you going to encourage this week? Resolve to use your influence to encourage someone to carry out an act of love or a good work this week.

KEY VERSE v24

'No one can serve two masters. Either you will hate the one and love the other, or you will be devoted to the one and despise the other.'

SO, IT BOILS down to this. This is the bottom line – the final page of Part One of our topic 'Peer Pressure'. No one can serve two masters. Peer pressure is all about choices – big choices, little choices, easy choices, complicated choices – yet just choices. Peer pressure tries to take away our ability to make our own decisions, by pressurising us to decide based on what others think or do.

Today's key verse makes it clear that this isn't a good way to live. We can either be people who make our decisions based on our faith, or we can be people who make our decisions based on the actions and influences of others. On paper, this might seem to be an obvious choice – the right answer just jumps off the page. However, in practice we know that it isn't always that easy.

There'll be some days when we make the right choice – our decisions are based on what we know God would want. On other days, we'll be desperate to do what our friends do and will let our choices be influenced by our peers. What we should be striving for is more days when God is directing our path than days when it's the people around us who are directing us.

PRAY
Dear God, help me to make my choices based on what You would want, rather than on what the people around me would choose. Amen.

READ:
JOHN 10:1–10

KEY VERSE
V10

'I have come that they may have life, and have it to the full.'

PT1
HÜMOUR

HUMOUR IS A strange and wonderful thing. It can be very difficult to explain and everyone has a different idea of what's funny. What one person laughs at just leaves another confused. But humour and laughter make life richer and more enjoyable. Somehow, humour also seems to reflect something of God's character, and of His plan for us.

There are lots of different types of humour; think for a moment about what you find funny. Humour can include pun, sarcasm or slapstick, be observational,

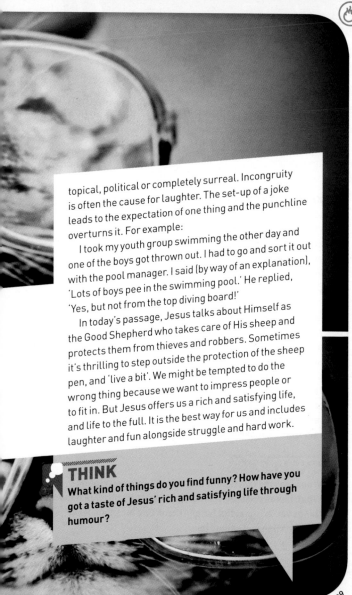

topical, political or completely surreal. Incongruity is often the cause for laughter. The set-up of a joke leads to the expectation of one thing and the punchline overturns it. For example:

I took my youth group swimming the other day and one of the boys got thrown out. I had to go and sort it out with the pool manager. I said (by way of an explanation), 'Lots of boys pee in the swimming pool.' He replied, 'Yes, but not from the top diving board!'

In today's passage, Jesus talks about Himself as the Good Shepherd who takes care of His sheep and protects them from thieves and robbers. Sometimes it's thrilling to step outside the protection of the sheep pen, and 'live a bit'. We might be tempted to do the wrong thing because we want to impress people or to fit in. But Jesus offers us a rich and satisfying life, and life to the full. It is the best way for us and includes laughter and fun alongside struggle and hard work.

THINK

What kind of things do you find funny? How have you got a taste of Jesus' rich and satisfying life through humour?

READ:
ECCLESIASTES 3:9–14

KEY VERSE v12

'there is nothing better for people than to be happy and to do good while they live.'

KARL BARTH ONCE said, 'Laughter is the closest thing to the grace of God.'[1] I believe that positive, life-affirming laughter brings us closer to knowing something of the love and acceptance of a God who created us to enjoy life through everything He made. Author Tom Mullen writes, 'If humour and laughter are gifts from God … losing the ability to laugh is poor stewardship.'[2]

Comedian Ken Dodd allegedly describes laughter as 'a noise that comes out of a hole in your face – anywhere else and you're in big trouble'. Laughter happens when we are caught out unexpectedly and something happens that surprises us.

When we are busy and under pressure from school or family expectations sometimes we don't make enough time to relax, enjoy life and have a really good laugh. Laughter is created by God to remind us of the joy He has in us. It's important to make time for it.

CHALLENGE

When was the last time you had a really big belly laugh? What makes you laugh? What lightens your spirit? List the things you are grateful for and thank God for them. Make time to laugh and enjoy life.

[1] http://www.experiencefestival.com/a/Inspirational_Quotes/id/223700
[2] Tom Mullen, *Laughing Out Loud and Other Religious Experiences* (Texas: Word Books, 1983) p26

KEY VERSE V42

'They devoted themselves to the apostles' teaching and to fellowship, to the breaking of bread and to prayer.'

IF YOU HAVE ever been on a residential with your friends, your church or youth group, you will know that something funny always happens during those few days that people will talk about for years to come. 'Do you remember when …?'

When people share lives and community is built, even for a limited time, humour is guaranteed. This must also have been the case with the disciples and early Christians as they shared fellowship together.

Tom Mullen writes, 'Those who share a laugh together are, for the moment at least, brothers and sisters … Shared humour becomes the shared experience, and relationships are nurtured by celebrating words and deeds that induce another to laugh.'[1] Laughter brings people together despite differences. It may not solve problems or resolve conflicts but it helps people unite and trust one another. Out of this, relationships are built. The opposite can also be true. If someone is outside of the joke, they can feel excluded and isolated.

THINK

How much of your humour involves 'in-jokes' which exclude people outside your immediate circle of friends? How can you use humour in a way that brings people together and builds community and trust?

[1] Tom Mullen, *Laughing Out Loud and Other Religious Experiences* (Texas: Word Books, 1983) pp41–44

READ:
ECCLESIASTES 3:1–8

KEY VERSE V4

'a time to weep and a time to laugh'

LIFE IS FULL of ups and downs and sometimes it is easier to walk away from God when things are tough, because we don't understand why He allows us to suffer.

In this passage however, we read that feeling down is normal and even something to be expected. Indeed the Psalms, like Ecclesiastes here, are full of the breadth and depth of emotion – from pain to joy, and from anger with God to rejoicing. This is what it means to be fully human.

There seems to be a tendency within Christian circles to think that because you are a Christian all should be well, so sometimes we pretend that everything is 'just fine, thanks', when actually we are struggling with an issue or with God.

Is there an area of your life with which you are hurting or struggling right now? Are you feeling the need to pretend everything is 'just fine'? It's OK and normal to struggle with life and faith sometimes. There is a time to cry just as much as there is a time to laugh, and it is often through the struggle that we learn the most about ourselves and about God.

CHALLENGE

Are you experiencing a 'time to cry' at the moment? Talk to a close friend or your youth leader about this. Remember that God is with us when we're hurting and you can take your struggles to Him too.

KEY VERSE V22

'A cheerful heart is good medicine, but a crushed spirit dries up the bones.'

PROVERBS IS A book of wise sayings and common sense on how to live a godly life. Verse 22 offers sound advice – there is medical evidence to suggest that laughter does speed up the recovery process.

There is a rich heritage of humour in the Jewish culture, perhaps due to the struggle and pain in their history. Messianic Jewish author Michele Guinness writes in her book *A Little Kosher Seasoning* (Hodder & Stoughton, 1994): 'Perhaps it is not the why of suffering which counts, but what we do with it. "Pain is inevitable," said one American writer, "but misery is optional." Positive action, channelling the emotional flood, seems to be a part of the healing process.'

Comedian Jimmy Carr echoes her thoughts, writing, 'Our ability to joke about things that are painful or forbidden is a valuable asset, a handle on sanity in a mad world. We tell jokes because human existence is an unforgiving slog; we tell them in the face of overwhelming odds and despite the ravages of time and fate.'[1]

CHALLENGE

Positive thinking is biblical. Instead of dwelling on the negative and moaning about what you haven't got or can't change, look on the bright side and try to focus on what's good in the situation or purpose. Live with hope – keep a cheerful heart.

[1] Jimmy Carr & Lucy Greeves, *The Naked Jape* (London: Penguin Books, 2006) p7

READ:
LUKE 6:17–36

KEY VERSE V21

'Blessed are you who weep now,
for you will laugh.'

I REMEMBER READING a book by Tony Campolo when I was younger, entitled *The Kingdom of God is a Party* (Thomas Nelson Publishers, 1992). It reminded me how exciting it will be to get to heaven; a place where God will wipe every tear from our eyes, and there will be no more death or sorrow or crying or pain. All these things will be gone forever (see Rev. 21:4). Heaven's not going to be full of chubby little baby-angels playing harps on clouds, like in some Victorian painting. It's going to be a place full of real joy and praise and celebration and laughter.

Exciting as this may be for our future, our job whilst here on earth is to seek to bring about God's kingdom in the here and now. We can be God's agents of change; people who bring His joy and comfort to others, particularly those who are hurting. Inspired by the knowledge that we are loved by God, we can bless other people with our words, deeds and humour. Through us, God can bless people who weep and help them laugh once more.

PRAY
Is there anyone you know who might need some encouragement today? Pray for an opportunity for God to bless them through you.

WEEKEND
1/2 OCT

KEY VERSE v25

'God made the wild animals according to their kinds, the livestock according to their kinds, and all the creatures that move along the ground according to their kinds. And God saw that it was good.'

WHEN GOD CREATED our world He said that it was 'good'. He created it for us to enjoy, to explore and also to take care of. Are you ever amazed by some of the weird creatures and plants in the world? Have you ever watched nature programmes and marvelled over how bizarre and really quite odd some of the creatures on our wonderful planet are? There's the blue-bottomed baboon, the duck-billed platypus, the long-nosed monkey, the aye-aye rodent and numerous other strange and wonderful creatures ... There's a massive amount to discover!

CONTINUED▶

So let's explore, let's decide to do everything we can to protect God's creation and let's appreciate how stunning the world is.

When was the last time you were struck by the pure joy and exuberance in the natural world? God created this world for you to enjoy. Take some time this weekend to notice the beauty around you and imagine God laughing with delight as He crafted it all. Thank Him for something of His creation, whether it's a flower growing up between the paving slabs in a city, crashing waves or rolling hills, volcanoes, the stars ... whatever it is in the universe that makes you just go, 'Wow!'.

PRAY

Take a walk through a park or some woods or along a beach. Walk slowly. Look around you and be open to new insights. Notice the beauty and detail in God's creation, thank Him for what He has made and share in His joy.

KEY VERSE V4

'The One enthroned in heaven laughs;
the Lord scoffs at them.'

WE MIGHT WISH it otherwise, but the only direct reference to God laughing in the Bible is God seeming to laugh in cruel judgment of people who don't acknowledge Him. This may sound harsh, but it is the arrogant and self-serving who are the targets of God's laughter. As Tal Bonham puts it, 'It is tragically hilarious to the mind of God that human beings, who owe God everything, are willing to pay Him nothing – not even the admission of His existence.'[1] God's agenda for using humour seems to be to expose folly and hypocrisy and to puncture human pride.

But this laughter does not come from afar. It comes from a God who wants to be involved and, indeed, who came in the person of Jesus and knows the human pain of being rejected, insulted and betrayed. God laughing at those who do not know Him must be seen in the light of God's salvation and grace.

There is still plenty here to challenge us though. We believe in a God who knows and cares for us and has a plan for our lives. But sometimes we still waste our time making plans of our own, without bothering with God's perspective. This is laughable to God!

THINK

How can we avoid having God laugh at us? How can we make sure we acknowledge Him and involve Him in our plans and decisions?

[1] Tal Bonham, *Humour: God's Gift* (Tennessee: Broadman Press, 1988) p18

READ:
GENESIS 18:12-25

KEY VERSE V12

'So Sarah laughed to herself as she thought, "After I am worn out and my lord is old, will I now have this pleasure?"'

THE IDEA OF having a baby was laughable to Sarah. She was 75, well past the usual age for having children, and her husband was even older. The idea seemed so ridiculous, she couldn't help laughing to herself.

Sarah doubted that even God could make something this incredible happen. But God responded, 'Why did Sarah laugh and say, "Will I really have a child, now that I am old?" Is anything too hard for the Lord?' (vv13–14).

When Sarah eventually gave birth (she was probably 92 then, according to the Bible and some mathematicians), she called the baby Isaac, meaning 'he who laughs'. Perhaps she learned through this experience that God's plans are never laughable, however unlikely they seem. Certainly, she knew that God had brought her joy (see Gen. 21:6–7).

Is anything too hard for the Lord? How often do we, like Sarah, doubt God and His plans for our lives? It's often all too easy to lack trust in God and even become a bit cynical about His care for us. When that happens, we try with all our efforts to sort things in our own strength and all it does is make us tired and anxious.

PRAY

In which areas of your life are you cautious about trusting God? Are you finding yourself doubting that God will act? Ask God now to help you trust Him more in those things and reassure you of His love and trustworthiness.

KEY VERSE v22

'Even the handle sank in after the blade, and his bowels discharged. Ehud did not pull the sword out, and the fat closed in over it.'

THIS KING OF Moab had everything and lived a life of excess. But God was not happy with his priorities and the way he was oppressing the Israelites. Eglon, the king, is a caricature; a figure of ridicule and humour. He is so fat that even the handle of the dagger is enveloped in his obese belly. He then proceeds to explode his bowels all over the floor and he is not found immediately because his servants assume he is on the toilet.

Eglon's obesity can be taken to represent greed, pleasure seeking, self-centredness and a lack of self-control. In God's eyes, all this was unacceptable. These attitudes are unacceptable for us, too.

We live in the affluent West, where it is said that by 2040, we will consume 65% of the world's energy resources.[1] And there are currently 3.7 million children living in poverty in the UK.[2] How much 'stuff' do you own? How many of your possessions are really necessary? Mother Theresa once said, 'Live simply so that others may simply live.'

→ CHALLENGE

Have a clear out and give some of the 'stuff' you don't need to a charity shop. As you go through your wardrobe or cupboards, pray for those who are living in poverty.

[1] www.theatlantic.com/technology/archive/2013/12/heres-why-developing-countries-will-consume-65-of-the-worlds-energy-by-2040/282006/
[2] www.barnardos.org.uk/what_we_do/our_work/child_poverty/child_poverty_what_is_poverty/child_poverty_statistics_facts.html

READ:
NUMBERS 22:21–41

KEY VERSE V28

'Then the LORD opened the donkey's mouth, and it said to Balaam, "What have I done to you to make you beat me these three times?"'

A TALKING DONKEY? God does choose original and humorous ways to communicate to us humans, doesn't He? And the weird thing is that Balaam didn't seem to bat an eyelid that his donkey spoke to him! God had to go to extremes to get through to Balaam, because Balaam seemed so determined to ignore Him. God had already spoken to Balaam directly and told him not to go and curse the Israelites (v12), but Balaam had chosen to go anyway.

God may not speak to you through a donkey, but how do you hear His voice and guidance in your life? Much of the time God 'speaks' through the Bible as we pray and study it, but when and how do you take time to listen? How often are you still and quiet enough to let God get a word in? And how willing are you to follow God's lead when you do hear His voice? It's very dangerous to get into Balaam's position and directly disobey God. Balaam comes alarmingly close to being killed (v33)! Let's not make God go to extremes to get through to us, however amusing that might seem at the time.

PRAY

Spend some time in silence today, perhaps lighting a candle to mark the time. Ask God to speak to you and help you to hear His voice clearly. Give Him space to speak, listen to what He has to say and then act on it.

KEY VERSE V27

'About noontime Elijah began mocking them. "You'll have to shout louder," he scoffed, "for surely he is a god! Perhaps he is daydreaming, or is relieving himself."' (NLT)

MORE TOILET HUMOUR! Elijah suggests that maybe Baal, the god worshipped by the people of Israel, is not answering their prayers because he is on the toilet. Elijah is courageous enough and confident enough in God that he ridicules the prophets of Baal. He even goes as far as pouring water over the unlit wood before asking God to bring down fire to light it. Is he mad? Or does he just have much greater faith than I would, were I to find myself in that situation?

When we pray, how confident are we that God will answer our prayers and do something? Do we pray with the confidence that Elijah had or do we pray half-hearted prayers, not really expecting God to answer them? That is a huge challenge, particularly at the times when we don't see immediate answers to our prayers.

I once prayed for healing for a friend of mine with agonising back pain. The physical pain did not ease and I was left feeling both disappointed and frustrated with God. It was years later when she told me that it wasn't really physical healing that she needed. She said she had needed internal healing, and God answered that prayer, starting that night.

PRAY

It may be that you sometimes get disheartened or frustrated with God when you don't see immediate answers. But persevere. Remember Elijah's faith and courage and ask God to help you trust Him more.

41

READ:
JAMES 4:1–10

KEY VERSE
V7

'Submit yourselves, then, to God.'

PT1
OBEDIENCE

OBEDIENCE IS NOT fashionable. In many ways, our culture urges us to do what we want; to insist on our rights, make ourselves comfortable and ignore anyone who tells us to do things their way. The idea of obeying someone else – not just listening to that person, but constantly obeying them – can seem strange to people around us. But this is Jesus' way. Following Jesus means doing what God wants, not what we want. It means serving other people, not ourselves, and focusing on our responsibilities, not our rights.

Obeying someone can feel uncomfortable. Submitting to anyone can sound like a very negative concept. Choosing to submit to someone makes us vulnerable to that person hurting us and taking advantage of us. So why is it a good thing for us to submit to God? In the next two weeks, we'll explore some answers to this question and think about exactly what obeying God means for us.

For now, these verses from James reassure us that God can be trusted. As we come to God and let Him rule our lives, He will come close to us (v8), and if we choose to make ourselves humble, He will honour us. We can trust God to care for us and do what is best for us. So we needn't be afraid to submit to Him, obey Him and make ourselves vulnerable to Him. God loves us, wants to bless us and only wants to be in control of us because His plans are always better than our own.

▲ PRAY

Ask God to show you what obeying Him really means. Be patient, listen and see what He has to say. Choose to submit to Him, even if that takes you outside your comfort zone.

READ:
JOB 22:21-30

KEY VERSE V21

'Submit to God and be at peace with him;
in this way prosperity will come to you.'

AT FIRST LOOK, this verse seems to say that God is like a vending machine. If you put a coin in a vending machine, out comes a chocolate bar. If you submit to God, out comes peace, happiness and an easy life. So does this verse really mean that if we obey God, life will always be easy? Of course not!

Living for God is about having a relationship with Him, not about what we can get out of Him. And God certainly doesn't guarantee us an easy life. Many of us know people who have chosen to submit to God completely and then faced some really hard times. We might even have experienced that ourselves. But our key verse does reassure us that God's way is always the best way.

Submitting to God won't necessarily make us rich, famous or popular but, even if life is hard, we will find true peace and real purpose if we obey Him wholeheartedly.

CHALLENGE

Are you obeying God wholeheartedly? Or are you holding back in case He asks you to do something you don't really want to do? Choose today to submit to God, whatever happens. Remember, you can trust Him!

KEY VERSE v5

'we've worked hard all night and haven't caught anything. But because you say so, I will let down the nets.'

YOU MIGHT KNOW that the first electric light bulb was invented by Thomas Edison. What you might not know is that Edison got through hundreds of unsuccessful designs before finally producing a working light bulb in October 1879. There must have been days when trying another slightly different design must have seemed to Edison like the last thing he should do. Trying something completely different or just giving up would have seemed far wiser. And yet, he persevered – and the result was something amazing. The disciples might have felt similarly. They had fished all night and caught nothing. To repeat almost exactly what they'd been doing already made no sense at all! But even though Peter knew very little about Jesus, he realised that Jesus had real authority, so he trusted Him. When Peter acts on his trust and does what Jesus says, the results are amazing. Obeying Jesus means doing what He says, even when it doesn't immediately seem wise. Jesus can give us new insights for tough situations. Sometimes this might mean a surprising new option. At other times, it might just mean carrying on when we feel like giving up. Either way, if we obey Jesus, we can trust His way to be the wisest. The results can be spectacular!

THINK

What are you struggling with at the moment? What might Jesus be saying about how to solve the problem?

READ:
MATTHEW 22:34–40

KEY VERSE v40

'All the Law and the Prophets hang on these two commandments.'

OCCASIONALLY, IF I'M feeling romantic, I'll buy my wife a bunch of flowers. Most mornings, I'll get up and make her a cup of tea, then take it to her in bed. On Saturdays I take my son out for a while, to give my wife some time to herself. And I make sure that I always spend at least one evening a week with her and no one else.

It might sound like my relationship with my wife is simply a list of stuff to do. Of course, there's far more to it than that. I don't do these things just for the sake of doing them, or because I think I ought to. I do them because I love my wife and I want to make her happy. As I've got to know her, I've realised that doing things like this makes her happy.

Living for God is similar to this. It's about far more than doing what look like good things and not doing what look like bad things: it's about getting to know and love Him. As we get closer to God, we will find ourselves wanting to do what pleases Him. Obeying God can actually be very simple. If our aim is to love Him and to love the people He's created, we won't wander far from what He wants of us.

PRAY
Father God, help me to love You and Your people. Let my life show that I love You and want to do things Your way. Amen.

KEY VERSE V24

'But let justice roll on like a river, righteousness like a never-failing stream!'

IT'S OBVIOUS, NOT just from these verses but from many different passages in the Bible, that God is passionate about justice. Justice – care for the poor and marginalised – is a thread which runs the whole way through the Bible. Justice is a cornerstone of the books of the Law. When the prophets spoke God's words to Israel and Judah, they urged the people to exercise justice for those who needed it. A hallmark of Jesus' ministry was caring for the sick, the poor and the outcasts. If we truly want to obey God, our lives should be characterised by caring for the needy too.

This will probably mean slightly different things for each of us. It might mean helping out at your local homeless shelter, regularly donating money to an international development charity like Tearfund, or even taking a year out to be part of a project helping poor people in the developing world. It might just mean befriending the person in your class who nobody else will talk to. But whatever it means for us, if we want to obey God, we have to take justice seriously.

PRAY
Ask God what He wants you to do to bring a little more of His justice into the world. Listen to what He has to say. Then obey!

READ:
PROVERBS 3:1–12

KEY VERSE v6

'in all your ways submit to him, and he will make your paths straight.'

I'VE ALWAYS LOVED music, particularly rock. When I was a teenager, I had the uneasy feeling that some of the bands I was listening to weren't good for me. In my heart of hearts, I knew God didn't really want me listening to this stuff. For a while, I ignored this feeling. The uneasy feeling wasn't going away, though, so I decided to do something about it and gave away some of my CDs. I didn't completely stop listening to rock music – I still enjoy it now – but I did stop listening to bands that were having a negative effect on the way I thought. I realised that if I wanted to live for God, I had to obey Him in everything, including the music I listened to.

We might think it's OK to keep one or two areas of life off-limits to God, as long as we're obeying Him in everything else. The problem is, a bad decision in one area of life can have a big impact on your whole life. Drinking too much or experimenting with drugs can make a mess of our health, our finances and our faith. And it's so easy to wander away from God because of an unwise relationship. It's important to obey God in every decision we make. If we do that, He will always show us the best way.

CHALLENGE

Is there any area of your life that you've been trying to keep God away from? Now's the time to let Him in!

WEEKEND

READ:
DEUTERONOMY 11:8–28

KEY VERSE V26

'See, I am setting before you today a blessing and a curse'

WE WERE ATTEMPTING the Three Peaks Challenge – climbing the highest mountains in Scotland, England and Wales in 24 hours. We'd already managed Ben Nevis, in the Scottish Highlands, and at 4am we made a start on England's Scafell Pike. Near the foot of the mountain, the path ran along the bank of a river. We knew we needed to cross the river using a ford, but it was dark, and we couldn't see where we were supposed to cross. So we kept going along the path. It seemed like the sensible option.

CONTINUED▸▸

We knew we were in trouble when the path became less clear, the mountain got steeper and we had to start scrambling on all fours. We checked the map and realised we were well off course. We'd missed the ford and made a bad decision to keep going. As a result of this, every step had taken us further from where we should have been. It left us in a huge mess and by the time we'd retraced our steps, we had no chance of completing the challenge within the time limit.

Often, we can't see the consequences of a little compromise. Making a small selfish decision, even if it seems sensible at the time, can eventually lead us a long way from where God wants us. It puts us on the way to a lot of pain and frustration. Obeying God will bring blessings, because His way is always wisest. Going our own way, even in a small decision, brings a curse, not because God is waiting to strike us down, but because we're wandering away from God and the good plans He has for us. The choice is yours.

THINK

Are you compromising on anything God wants you to do? Spend some time reflecting on this. If God calls anything to mind, ask for His forgiveness and His help to get back on track.

KEY VERSE V3

'But Jonah ran away from the LORD and headed for Tarshish.'

HAVE YOU EVER tried to take a cat to see the vet? Generally, when the cat sees you coming towards him with a basket, he'll work out what's going on, get scared, run in the opposite direction and disappear from view. You'll probably find him half an hour later, hiding behind the sofa. The cat is just delaying the inevitable, of course. It's only a matter of time before you find him, cram him into the basket and get him to the vet. Resisting you is a waste of time.

In these verses, we find Jonah behaving like the cat. It was absolutely clear to Jonah what God wanted him to do. But he decided that he didn't like this idea and ran away. The key verse tells us that Jonah wasn't just running away from God's plan, he was running away from God Himself! How ridiculous! We can see that God would find Jonah wherever he went. We'd never behave like that, would we? Or maybe we would. We can sometimes feel like going our own way, especially when God's way looks scary. But God will never let us go, and He has a habit of accomplishing something when He's decided on it. Jonah found this out after spending three days inside a fish and being spat out onto a beach!

CHALLENGE

Honesty time: has God told you to do something which would take you outside your comfort zone? Are you obeying Him in this? If so, good for you. If not, ask for His help, take a deep breath and go for it.

READ:
1 SAMUEL 10:1–8

KEY VERSE V7

'do whatever your hand finds to do, for God is with you.'

DO YOU EVER tie yourself in knots, trying to work out what God wants you to do – even in making tiny decisions? 'Hmmm ... Shreddies or Weetabix for breakfast today? Or maybe God wants me to have Corn Flakes ... or Coco Pops. Argh!'

Yesterday, we thought about how to respond when God's will isn't 100 per cent clear. On the other hand, sometimes God just lets us choose what to do. God loves us enough to give us free will; the ability to make choices for ourselves. Sometimes, obeying God just means using our common sense and making a choice for ourselves, particularly when it's a small and insignificant decision. Fretting over what God wants us to eat for breakfast or what He wants us to wear today just isn't worth it!

Obviously we need to be careful with this idea. Our habit should be to listen to God, not to automatically do our own thing. But if we're honestly trying to obey God, we won't go far wrong. If we're open to His leading, God sometimes lets us do whatever we think is right.

CHALLENGE
Is a small decision giving you a headache? Relax, use your common sense and do whatever you think is right. God is with you!

KEY VERSE v33

'But seek first his kingdom and his righteousness, and all these things will be given to you as well.'

LIFE BOMBARDS US with so many things to worry about. It's easy to let worries about money, work, dating and all sorts of other stuff distract us from what really matters in life. A few years ago, I was worrying about my future, particularly my lack of career plans and lack of a girlfriend. About this time, I ran into a friend who gave me some wise advice: 'Put following God first. He'll take care of everything else.' My friend was right. I did my best to live for God in the years that followed, and all the stuff I'd been worrying about gradually fell into place.

If we're set on obeying God, life won't always be easy – in fact, sometimes it will be hard. However, we'll have the satisfaction of knowing that we're working with someone who loves us utterly and forever, and for something good, purposeful and that will last for eternity. Above all, there's no need to worry! If we put God and His plans first, we can trust Him to take care of everything we need.

PRAY

What do you worry about? Pray about these things, ask God to take care of them and resolve to follow Him, wherever He takes you.

READ:
JOHN 17:9-10

KEY VERSE
V9

'I am not praying for the world, but for those you have given me'

PT2
DISCIPLE-
SHIP

WELCOME BACK TO our study on discipleship and tips on living for Jesus. What does it mean to be a disciple? In today's reading, Jesus is praying for those who know Him. Not for everybody in the whole world, but specifically for those He has spent time with, and especially the ones who know Him personally – the disciples who were with Him then and His disciples now ... that's you, me and other Christians in our day and age.

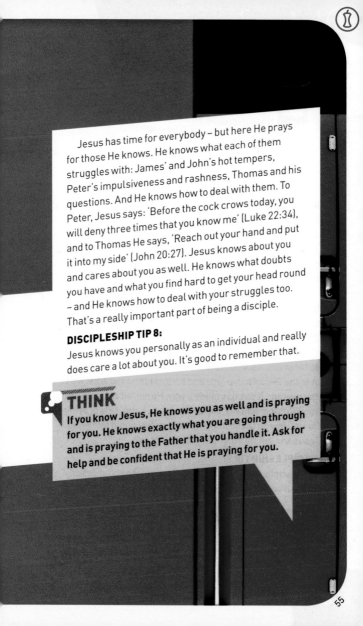

Jesus has time for everybody – but here He prays for those He knows. He knows what each of them struggles with: James' and John's hot tempers, Peter's impulsiveness and rashness, Thomas and his questions. And He knows how to deal with them. To Peter, Jesus says: 'Before the cock crows today, you will deny three times that you know me' (Luke 22:34), and to Thomas He says, 'Reach out your hand and put it into my side' (John 20:27). Jesus knows about you and cares about you as well. He knows what doubts you have and what you find hard to get your head round – and He knows how to deal with your struggles too. That's a really important part of being a disciple.

DISCIPLESHIP TIP 8:
Jesus knows you personally as an individual and really does care a lot about you. It's good to remember that.

THINK
If you know Jesus, He knows you as well and is praying for you. He knows exactly what you are going through and is praying to the Father that you handle it. Ask for help and be confident that He is praying for you.

READ:
JOHN 17:21–26

KEY VERSE v26

'I have made you known to them, and will continue to make you known'

IF GOD HAS been revealed to you by Jesus, what are you going to do about it? Today's chapter ends with a promise from Jesus: He will continue to reveal Himself. We know that this prayer is not just for the disciples way back then, but for us as disciples now. Jesus has promised to keep on revealing more and more of God to us.

As disciples, we have been given the challenge to pass on the knowledge to our friends, family and those around us. It sounds really hard, but with Jesus on our side, is it really that difficult?

Let's look back at what we've learned about discipleship so far in this issue of *Mettle*. Think about all you've read. Go over the Discipleship Tips and try to understand what we've discovered: Jesus has made a way, He has all authority, He knows us individually, He cares about us and He is praying for us. How do these things make you feel about following Jesus and telling other people about Him?

DISCIPLESHIP TIP 9:
As a disciple, desire every day to learn more about Jesus; then put what you discover into practice.

PRAY
Father, reveal more of Yourself today, so that I may be able to talk to others about You, the God who lives in me. Amen.

WEEKEND

READ:
PHILIPPIANS 1:27–28

KEY VERSE v27

'conduct yourselves in a manner worthy of the gospel of Christ.'

WHAT DO YOU do that is honouring to God? That's not a trick question to make you feel guilty. You may find there are more possibilities to live a life worthy of heaven than you realise.

Living a life for Jesus does not necessarily mean stopping the things we are involved in during everyday life. There's nothing wrong with playing football or dancing, for example. However, it will require checking that these things reflect our relationship with Jesus. So, if you play football, what is your attitude like when you play?

CONTINUED▶

▼ What about your language? If you dance, is it just to make yourself look good? Or do you dance as
▼ an act of worship to God and the abilities He has given you?
▼
▼ Whatever you do, it's an opportunity to honour God and point other people towards Him. Make the most of this opportunity. People around
▼ you may question why you consider Jesus in your actions. They may not understand your
▼ relationship with Him. Stand your ground, put God first and don't give in to pressure to live life as other people do.

▼
▼ **DISCIPLESHIP TIP 10:**
Find someone to talk to about the ups and downs of being a Christian. Encourage each other with what you can both do to honour God by your lifestyle, and pray together so that you can both stand firm in following Jesus.

CHALLENGE

Do you realise that you have been chosen to be a citizen of heaven? Jesus has set you apart for a life designed by Him that you can live out in all its fullness – to be worthy of an eternal life in the presence of Almighty God.

KEY VERSE v16

'You are the Messiah, the Son of the living God.'

HOW CAN AN encounter with Jesus change a person's life? Over the next four days we are going to look at different people from the Bible and try to answer this question.

First up is Peter. Peter was a Galilean fisherman when he met Jesus, a couple of years before he made the statement we read in verse 16. Peter had been through a lot in those years. He'd heard Jesus teach, he'd seen Jesus heal people, he'd helped Jesus feed the five thousand and he had even walked on water.

Peter first answered a call to follow Jesus, and only then was he able to be a part of these things. Our understanding of Jesus takes time to develop. To begin with we don't understand everything; it's through our experience and knowledge of Jesus that we really get to know Him. This does take time; and every so often we need to stop and be challenged about what we think and how it affects our life.

DISCIPLESHIP TIP 11:
Set yourself this objective: to know Jesus better today than you did yesterday and to know Him more tomorrow than you do today.

THINK
Where are you with Jesus? Where do you want to be?
Do you know Him better than you did yesterday?
Spend five minutes now in silence, just asking God to help you answer those questions.

READ:
MATTHEW 8:5–13

KEY VERSE V8

'Lord, I do not deserve to have you come under my roof. But just say the word, and my servant will be healed.'

NOW WE LOOK into the conduct of a Roman officer when he met Jesus. He knew about authority: 'I tell this one, "Go," and he goes; and that one, "Come," and he comes.' (v9). He himself was under the authority of Rome and his superior officers, and he held authority over his soldiers. He realised that Jesus had the power and authority of the One who sent Him. Jesus was the Son of God and therefore held the authority of God.

The officer knew the signs to look for: Jesus' conduct, the way Jesus spoke, the way He treated people and the way He commanded miracles. He recognised what he saw in Jesus and understood who Jesus was. He had complete faith that Jesus could heal his servant with just a word. Now add what Jesus said in John 14:12: 'whoever believes in me will do the works I have been doing, and they will do even greater things than these' and we can see that i f we follow Jesus, we have His power and authority too!

DISCIPLESHIP TIP 12:
You have great power through your faith in Jesus. Be willing to use it – pray for people and expect things to happen – great things!

CHALLENGE

Do you have faith like the Roman officer? Look back over the last six months. Can you think of times when you have really felt that God was involved in your life? Think about what you have learnt.

KEY VERSE V60

'Then he fell on his knees and cried out,
"Lord, do not hold this sin against them."
When he had said this, he fell asleep.'

THE THIRD INDIVIDUAL we're going to look at whose life was
powerfully impacted by Jesus, Stephen, was the first Christian
to be killed for his belief and defence of God. Here we find him
defending himself in front of the Sanhedrin (Jewish council of
leaders) against the charge of blasphemy. Stephen showed no
fear. He stood up for what he believed in and even asked God to
forgive them as they stoned him to death!

Stephen was utterly convinced that Jesus was the Son of
God – so much so that he was willing to die declaring it. When
was the last time you stood up for what you believed? I'm not
talking about forcing what you believe on someone but, when
challenged, do you actually say you are a Christian? And if
people are giving you a hard time for being a Christian, how
easy do you find it to forgive them?

DISCIPLESHIP TIP 13:
Being a disciple of Christ means that you have to learn to
forgive others. This can be difficult, particularly if something
really serious has happened, but with the help of the Holy
Spirit, forgiveness is possible.

THINK
Stephen made the ultimate sacrifice for what he believed.
How do you think he was able to do that?

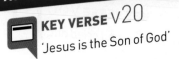

READ:
ACTS 9:1–25

KEY VERSE v20

'Jesus is the Son of God'

THE FINAL PERSON we are going to look at is Paul. When we first meet Paul at the stoning to death of Stephen, he is called Saul. He is out to get the Christians, as he believes that they are wrong in their belief in Jesus. He takes every opportunity to throw them into prison and to stir up trouble against them; he was 'eager to kill the Lord's followers'. He was a man on a mission!

Here we find him travelling to Damascus when he is hit by a brilliant beam of light. He is blinded and has a conversation with Jesus over the next three days. Then Ananias, a believer in Damascus, is sent by God to pray for Saul to regain his sight and to receive the Holy Spirit. Faithfully Ananias did this and Saul went on to be baptised and to boldly preach that Jesus was indeed the Son of God.

DISCIPLESHIP TIP 14:

Listen to others who are more experienced in following Jesus and be willing to open your heart as God reveals His character to you. God will never contradict what He says in the Bible.

THINK

Saul was convinced about Jesus and powerfully spoke to others – so much so that the Jewish leaders who'd originality invited him to speak decided to have him murdered.

KEY VERSE v15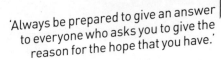

'Always be prepared to give an answer to everyone who asks you to give the reason for the hope that you have.'

WHY BELIEVE? WHAT would it take for some of your friends to believe in Jesus? I have often been in heated discussions with friends about Jesus being the Son of God, about Him being an historical figure and about His miracles, yet nothing I said would convince them – even historical facts. They still wanted to see Him as (at most) a nice guy who did some nice things. Crowds of people in Jesus' day saw Him do miracles, meet their practical needs and show real wisdom and intelligence in His answers to their questions. Yet still some questioned who He was.

St Francis of Assisi is known for the saying: 'Proclaim the Gospel at all times, and if necessary, use words.' By our actions people will see what we are like and will ask us questions about why we do what we do. Then we need to be able to answer those questions. Clever arguments are good, but it's when people can see our faith in action that they really get interested.

DISCIPLESHIP TIP 15:
Be ready to talk about why you are a Christian, but remember that you don't have to share everything all at once. Ask God to show you the right thing to say at the right time.

THINK
Can you tell your story of why and how you became a Christian? Try saying it out loud to yourself. As you do, ask yourself: 'Do my words match my actions?'

READ:
PHILIPPIANS 1:20–24

KEY VERSE v20

'I eagerly expect and hope that I will in no way be ashamed, but will have sufficient courage so that now as always Christ will be exalted'

HAVE YOU EVER seen a real fanatic of anything? They do everything to show how much of a 'fan' they are. They sing all the songs, wear the right clothes and spend all their money on the little 'extras' associated with whoever it is they are worshipping. However, the real crunch comes when their loyalty is tested. When a football team loses or a band brings out a rubbish song, some of their followers suddenly go quiet. But the true fans stand up for their beliefs even when they will be laughed at or ignored.

When do you struggle to be open about being a Christian? What is it that you worry will happen?

Facing these fears can allow you to experience really living for Christ.

Today's reading is from Paul's letter to the Christians in Philippi. He is struggling to decide which is better – to live for Christ or die for Christ. Not much of a choice, some might say. But here we have Paul arguing each way. For in his eyes, either way he is a winner. In death he will be with Christ; and in life he gets to tell more people about Christ. Perhaps as we get closer to God we realise that we can trust Him in any circumstances – and we find that we're then bolder in living for Him.

DISCIPLESHIP TIP 16:
Live for Christ boldly, so that you can tell others about Him and live your life in a way that honours Him.

PRAY
Tell God honestly why you sometimes struggle to be a Christian. Ask Him to help you to trust Him more, to overcome your struggles and to be strong enough to represent Jesus at all times.

READ:
1 THESSALONIANS 4:1–2

KEY VERSE V1

'live in order to please God, as in fact you are living. Now we ask you and urge you in the Lord Jesus to do this more and more.'

BEING A DISCIPLE of Christ is sometimes humdrum. Life goes on; it can even get into a rhythm and, before you know it, you have let things slip. You stop reading your Bible: this could be the first time in days you have picked up these notes. Nothing drastic has happened in your life, so you allow Jesus to slip out. Sure, He still has His place on Sundays, but the rest of the week ...?

Challenge yourself and remember: God loves to see you living a life for Him; He delights in watching you stand up for Him. To survive the challenges of being a Christian, don't settle for the good, but stretch yourself for the great.

No matter how much of Jesus you have in your life, He has more to offer you. Keep asking Him for more, and keep on doing the things He has planned for your life. Be careful not to live a life pleasing to God today, only to live without Him tomorrow. God wants you today, tomorrow and forever.

DISCIPLESHIP TIP 17:
Be encouraged to keep going. Put Jesus at the centre of what you do every day.

PRAY
Ask God to equip you for the long journey ahead with Him. Let Him know you want a life with Jesus forever – not just while it's fun.

KEY VERSE V19

'holding on to faith and a good conscience'

WHAT WORK DO you do each day? Do you work hard? Do you apply yourself to the jobs ahead of you every day?

Timothy had a vital job ahead of him. He had been given the task of leading a church. This was a very important role and he was a young man entrusted with it. Paul gave him all sorts of advice on the practical daily tasks he would have to fulfil. However, in the middle of all this practical advice, Paul tells Timothy the crucial ingredient in working for God: 'Cling tightly to your faith. Keep your actions clean and your conscience clear.'

Paul and Timothy had a close relationship and often wrote to each other. Paul's advice for Timothy was simply to trust in Jesus first. On 6 September, we considered mentoring. If you haven't yet got someone to talk to, think about it again and see if you could ask someone you know and trust to become your mentor.

DISCIPLESHIP TIP 18:

If we stay close to Jesus in our work, we can serve Him in everything we do, even if it at first seems to be nothing to do with Him.

PRAY

Father, thank You for all You have done for me. Help me to keep close to You in everything I do, today and all this week. Amen.

READ:
NEHEMIAH 2:11–20

KEY VERSE v18

'I also told them about the gracious hand of my God on me'

GREAT LEADERS ARE often only recognised after they have achieved success. Once everyone can see what they were trying to achieve then they can be appreciated for their determination and effort.

However, most leaders have made their plans for success long before anyone sees the outcome of their efforts. We see this in today's reading, where we hear from Nehemiah about the plan God has laid on his heart to rebuild the wall of Jerusalem – a plan that he achieves.

As a disciple of Christ, God has plans for you. He may give those plans only to you. You may not understand why He has chosen you to do a certain task, but God wants to be with you in your work. He wants to equip you to serve Him in whatever you are doing. Any work – be it at school, college, university, at home or in a job – can be an opportunity to serve God.

DISCIPLESHIP TIP 19:
Great opportunities to serve God cannot always be seen, but there are small ones around us every day – all we need to do is keep our eyes open to see them, even in the places and situations we wouldn't normally think of.

CHALLENGE
How can you serve God today? If you are struggling to think of anything, ask Him to open your eyes to the opportunities around you.

KEY VERSE V19

'So that your trust may be in the LORD,
I teach you today, even you.'

TODAY WE HAVE a list that some Bible translations head up as 'Sayings of the Wise' – this is good old fashioned discipleship advice from the Old Testament. If you have time, read on into chapter 23. God loves a diligent worker. He doesn't respond to people who just sit around and wait all day for someone else to do all the hard work. God will honour those who work hard at the tasks they are given.

Often we may feel as if we are not being rewarded for our efforts, and we see others being rewarded, apparently for no effort at all. (Have you ever wondered exactly why people make such a fuss over reality TV contestants?) Hold on to God's promise. He sees all our efforts and is not interested in the small rewards we can receive from those around us. God will reward those who go about their work without seeking glory or praise.

DISCIPLESHIP TIP 20:
If you have been given a job, then take your reward from knowing that you are working for God.

PRAY
Ask God to give you the energy and drive to try your best in your work. Ask Him to remind you each day that it is not for congratulations that we do good things.

READ:
1 PETER 2:4-10

KEY VERSE V9

'you are a chosen people, a royal priesthood, a holy nation, God's special possession, that you may declare the praises of him who called you out of darkness'

TODAY WE COME to the end of this section on discipleship. Having considered many of the ways in which we can live for God, the final thing to consider is why we are where we are.

Serving Jesus doesn't require travelling to the far ends of the earth and living in a tent (although it's possible God may ask you to do that in the future …)! You are most probably surrounded by people whose only knowledge of Jesus is the example they see in you. So wherever you are, you're in an important place.

Where you are now, your efforts to include Jesus in everything you do are the loudest and most effective example of Christ anybody could give to those around you. God has called you out of darkness into His wonderful light and has set you as His representative – His priest – in everything you do. Your friends and your family see Jesus through you.

DISCIPLESHIP TIP 21:
Remember that you're God's representative. Everything you do can show more of Him to people around you.

PRAY
Ask God to strengthen you to be a good example of Jesus in your work, your family and your community. Ask Him to prepare you for the conversations that may arise from your example.

READ:
ROMANS 12:1–5

KEY VERSE
V2

'Do not conform to the pattern of this world, but be transformed by the renewing of your mind.'

PT2 PEER PRESSURE

OVER THE NEXT two weeks, we're returning to the theme of peer pressure. Previously we've spent some time thinking about what peer pressure is and where it comes from. We've thought about what it might pressure us into doing, and how it can sometimes be used for positive ends. All in all, we've got a good handle on what the problem is. The trouble is: that's not where the issue ends.

CONTINUED▶▶

We would almost certainly be worried if, when we went to the doctor, the doctor told us what was wrong with us but then said nothing about a cure or a treatment. Knowing there's an obstacle we're going to have to face is half the battle, but the other half is knowing how to deal with that obstacle when the time comes. So, over the next couple of weeks we're going to look at what advice the writers of the Bible give us about how to deal with peer pressure.

Today's verse sets the starting point for our approach. Paul writes to the church in Rome, telling them very clearly that the way in which they act and think should be obviously different from the actions and thoughts of the world around them. As Christians, there are some things we shouldn't be a part of: joining in with peer pressure is one of those things. The question we're going to consider is: how do we free ourselves from the effects and influences of peer pressure? It's not an easy one to answer, but it's worth us having a go.

PRAY

Dear Lord, help me to be honest about the pressure people around me place upon me. Help me to think about how I can resist this pressure. Amen.

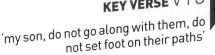
DON'T TOUCH! I wonder how many times we've seen a similar warning. There's something about human nature that, when we see a sign like this, our first thought is to do exactly the opposite! Many of us often find it very hard to heed a warning – no matter how loudly it's uttered.

Today's Bible verse tries to do just that – issue a warning, loud and clear. 'Stay away!' the writer warns. There are people who will try to lead you to do things that aren't good. This is a good place to start when thinking about how best to deal with peer pressure – steer clear!

If we know people who make a habit of dragging others into the trouble they're caught up in, it might be best to stay away from them. Now, this might be easier said than done, since often the things we ought to stay away from are the most tempting. Like the 'Don't Touch!' sign, things we know aren't good can have an unusual attraction. Sometimes we hang around with people we know will get us into trouble, but the bottom line is that they are going to drag us into things we shouldn't be doing – and we need to avoid that. Today's verse is a simple warning, but one we need to heed: 'Stay away!'

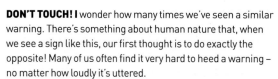

THINK

Who or what do you need to turn your back on? What are you being led into that you need to steer clear of? Be honest with God and with yourself.

READ:
MATTHEW 5:13–16

KEY VERSE V15

'Neither do people light a lamp and put it under a bowl. Instead they put it on its stand'

TODAY'S BIBLE VERSES might be quite well known to us. Sunday schools and youth groups often choose to teach on the theme of salt and light. My experience is that although we enjoy the activities and games which often feature as part of these sessions, we very rarely appreciate the meaning behind these words.

We are called to be like a light in the darkness. I imagine those listening to Jesus' words about light would have laughed at how silly what He was suggesting sounded. Who in their right mind would take something as warming and reassuring as a light in a dark house and then hide it away where it was of no good to anyone?

The same is true of us. Because Jesus is in us, we shine in a dark world. Why would we hide ourselves away? We should let everyone see the difference Jesus can make. And what does this all have to do with peer pressure? Today's verses remind us that sometimes we are going to stand out – we're going to have to be the only light in a dark place. There are times when, no matter what everyone else around is doing, we're going to have to do something else. Are you up for the challenge?

PRAY
Dear Lord, help me to be light in a dark world, and not to bow to the pressure to hide my light. Amen.

KEY VERSE V33

'But seek first his kingdom and his righteousness, and all these things will be given to you as well.'

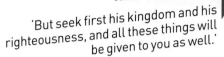

WHAT ARE YOUR priorities? Our lives are full of conflicting demands upon our time and energy. Do we prize being popular above all – or value fitting in more than anything else? What about money, fame and academic achievement: which of these do we want most?

The question of priorities is important. We only have so much time and energy – we can't give it to everything. So we put the most time and energy into what we see as the most important. If we want to be popular, then that is where we will devote our energies – bowing to peer pressure to make sure that we remain in favour.

If we listen to the many other social pressures in our world, we hear that money and fame are paramount. We will be tempted to invest our time and resources into securing them. However, today's Bible verse gives a heavenly perspective on the question of priorities. We are told to seek God's kingdom above all else. The rewards are clear, yet so is the cost. If we make this our number one goal, then we cannot devote our time and energy to pursuing the many other goals we are being pressured to achieve. And, if we give in to peer pressure, our energies are not being used to seek the kingdom of God.

→ CHALLENGE

Write your priorities down on a piece of paper. Spend some time with God being honest about your goals in life.

READ:
PHILIPPIANS 4:2–9

KEY VERSE V8

'Finally, brothers and sisters, whatever is true, whatever is noble, whatever is right ... think about such things.'

A HUGE CHUNK of secondary school Chemistry lessons are spent learning which test shows what. Rows of bottles are used in experiments to indicate the presence of a particular chemical or compound. If the substance goes this colour it is what you thought it was. If it goes that colour, it's not.

These tests help pupils to get a definite answer. Is it A or B, yes or no? Tests like this allow them to be sure whether they are right or not. Today's Bible verse introduces a different kind of indicator test. It's a test which tells us not what something's made of, but rather whether or not something is of God or not of God. These verses provide a good benchmark when we are being pressured into doing something.

Is what we're being pushed towards true, noble, right, pure, lovely, admirable, excellent or praiseworthy? If not, then it's probably something to avoid at all costs. It's not always 100% obvious whether something is true, noble, etc – and we'll look at how to deal with that in a few days' time. However, in the meantime, this can be a useful test when we're being pushed towards something. Does the test indicate it's something good or something we should avoid?

THINK
What are you doing at the moment that isn't true, noble, pure, lovely, admirable, excellent or praiseworthy? Should you stop doing it?

KEY VERSES vv1–2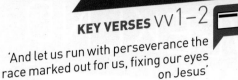

'And let us run with perseverance the race marked out for us, fixing our eyes on Jesus'

MANY OF YOU will have had the pleasure of taking part in a cross-country run at school. Whether through the local woods or around the school field, cross-country running is about stamina. For some, running long distances is not a problem and can even be quite good fun. But for many, the idea of running that far is not a nice one!

The first 200 metres are usually fine, then the next 200 metres may be all right, but after that it starts to get harder and harder – until it really becomes a case of mind over matter in order to finish the race. Today's Bible verse reminds us that living as a Christian can often be like this. Sometimes it's easy, but there will be times when it's tiring and draining, and it would be far easier to stop and have a sit down rather than carry on running.

When it comes to resisting peer pressure, it's also a case of endurance. It would be nice if once we'd said no that was it. However, the reality is that we have to keep on saying no; we have to continue to resist the pressure from those around us. It's going to be tiring, and it's going to be tempting to give up and give in to the pressure from those around us. But we must keep on going, for the finish line is one well worth reaching.

THINK

What do you do when resisting the peer pressure around you gets too much? How do you recharge so that you can keep on running?

READ:
1 THESSALONIANS 4:1–2

'Finally, dear brothers and sisters, we urge you in the name of the Lord Jesus to live in a way that pleases God' (NLT)

THERE'S ONE IN every class, in every school – someone who is desperate to please the teacher. All they want is to do what's right; to do what the teacher wants and to be recognised as having done the right thing. These people are often given a hard time by those around them – they get labelled 'teacher's pet' or worse. However, this name-calling often comes from a kind of jealousy. Secretly, most of us would quite like to be told that we've done a good job. We like to know that we've pleased the one in charge, and that they've noticed. We might not admit it, but it's a good feeling when the teacher notices that we've got it right.

Today's key verse is a request for us to please someone a bit more important than our Maths teacher.

It reminds us that we need to be living lives that please God – not because that's what gets us into heaven, but because why wouldn't we want to please the One who has given us so, so much?!

What's this got to do with peer pressure? Well, it gives us another tool to help us decide how to act. When thinking about whether to do what our friends want us to do – when we have to decide whether to conform or to stand out – we need to think about whether it will please God. We must also bear in mind that when we choose to please God, it's possible (or even likely) that we're going to get called names – but it will probably be because the name-callers have noticed what we have!

PRAY

Dear Lord, help me to always act in a way that will please You. Help me and guide me to make decisions that take me along paths that are good. Amen.

READ:
PROVERBS 22:24–25

KEY VERSES vv24–25

'Do not make friends with a hot-tempered person, do not associate with one easily angered, or you may learn their ways and get yourself ensnared.'

IF YOU'RE LUCKY enough to have younger brothers or sisters, or have friends with younger siblings, you'll know that they are swift to learn from those around them. You have to be very careful what you say and what you do around them, because they are quick to copy – and don't always copy the right things!

However, it's not only younger children who emulate the behaviour of those around them. Our peers can often be hugely influential in persuading us how to act or what to do. Today's Bible verse adds the next helpful piece of advice. If we know someone is going to teach us the wrong things, let's not hang around with them. No matter how much we think we can resist copying their behaviour, it might just be easier not to associate with them in the first place.

This can be hard, especially when it forces us to distance ourselves from people who are popular. However, if it stops us being pressured into things we are best out of, it might be better in the long run!

PRAY
Dear Lord, surround me with people who will build me up and will teach me to be more like Jesus. Help me to steer clear of people who will lead me into ways that take me away from You. Amen.

KEY VERSE V16

'keeping a clear conscience, so that those who speak maliciously against your good behaviour in Christ may be ashamed'

TUES 15 NOV

SCHOOLS, CHURCHES AND youth groups are all, whether we like it or not, prone to a little gossip. Something happens or someone does something, and very quickly everyone knows about it – and has said what they think about it.

Avoiding gossip is hard, and eliminating it is even harder, but today's verse gives us some helpful advice, especially when we apply it to the question of peer pressure. It reminds us of the importance of giving those around us as little fuel for gossip as possible.

People are going to talk about what you do and, if you stand up against peer pressure, they will probably talk about you all the more. However, if you've stood up for what you believe in, and you've done it with humility and gentleness rather than rubbing it in people's faces, today's verse assures us that those gossiping will soon realise that you are in the right.

Gossip can be a huge problem for groups, but if we stay strong and make sure our consciences are clear, we have nothing to worry about.

THINK

Do you gossip about others when they give in to peer pressure? Where and when do you find it hardest not to gossip about others?

READ:
JAMES 1:2–8

KEY VERSE V5

'If any of you lacks wisdom, you should ask God, who gives generously to all without finding fault, and it will be given to you.'

ALL OF US will know the best people to have on our team in a quiz. There are some people who are really good at knowing the right answers: they seem to have a gift for remembering things and applying what they know to the question being asked. Others of us find it much harder to choose the right answer: it might be this one or it might be that one.

Every day we're faced with pressures from all sides to do all sorts of things. Sometimes it's easy to spot the times when we're better off out of it – when we need to be strong and say no. But at other times it's a lot harder to discern whether it's OK to be doing it or not. Today's Bible verse reassures us that there's something we can do when we find ourselves in this situation.

Our God is a generous God, and He wants to help us do the right thing. We are not on our own when faced with tough decisions. We can ask God for wisdom to help us know when we need to stand firm and when it's OK to go with the flow. It's nice to know that there's Someone out there who will guide us.

CHALLENGE
Spend some time asking God for the wisdom you need. What is it you need to know? What are you not sure about?

THURS 17 NOV

KEY VERSE V13

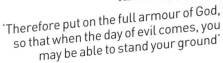

'Therefore put on the full armour of God, so that when the day of evil comes, you may be able to stand your ground'

IF YOU'VE EVER played any cricket, hockey or other such sport, you'll know that you need an awful lot of equipment in order to take part in the game. Some of this equipment makes playing the game easier (it would be pretty hard to play cricket without a cricket bat), and some of it makes playing the game safer (anyone who's played hockey without shin pads will appreciate why they're needed!).

Today's Bible verses tell us about a different type of equipment – equipment not for playing sport but for living as a Christian. It's often referred to as the armour of God and is our vital survival gear which offers us protection for our Christian journey.

The armour includes truth, peace, faith, salvation, God's righteousness and the Word of God – not quite a face guard, but far more useful when it comes to being a Christian. When facing issues such as peer pressure, if we pursue the truth, stay in a right relationship with God, seek peace, hang on to our faith, remember our salvation and use the Word of God, we'll find it easier to win the game. You shouldn't play sports without suitable equipment so we shouldn't start our day without the armour of God.

THINK

Which part of the equipment that God provides have you ignored and need to start using?

READ:
ROMANS 6:15–18

KEY VERSE v16

'Don't you know that when you offer yourselves to someone as obedient slaves, you are slaves of the one you obey ...?'

WE ENDED OUR first section on peer pressure thinking about choices, and that is where we finish again. Today's Bible verse gives a very clear message. We have a choice over what guides our thinking and, whatever we choose, we become a slave to it.

It sounds rather dramatic, and we might be tempted to dismiss this as over the top, but in reality it's all too true. When we give in to peer pressure, we become a slave to the ideas and actions of others. It's then possible that this slavery will end up getting us into trouble and will lead us along paths we wouldn't have chosen ourselves. However, we have another choice. We can resist the influences of those around us, no matter how fierce the pressure, and we can choose to obey God and seek His will for our lives.

God says He will help us do this by giving us wisdom, by helping us to know what is pure and what's not, by helping us to surround ourselves with people who won't pressure us into sin, and by helping us to resist the effects of the gossip and hardship that might follow. But despite all this, it comes down to a choice – who do you choose to obey?

CHALLENGE
Who do you obey? What are you a slave to? Are you happy with your answers?

READ:
JOSHUA 2:1-11

KEY VERSES
VV1-2

'Then Joshua son of Nun secretly sent two spies ... So they went and entered the house of a prostitute named Rahab and stayed there.'

PT2
HÜMOUR

IRONIC HUMOUR IS not laugh-out-loud funny, but it is very amusing when the opposite of a situation is said or done to make a point. When we take a closer look at Jesus' family tree, we find all sorts of less-than-perfect characters. From the line of Rahab, a prostitute who ran an inn in Jericho and hid Joshua's spies, came Jesus, the Son of God.

Rahab's family were spared when the Israelites conquered Jericho and she later went on to

CONTINUED▶▶

marry a man called Salmon, who was the great-great grandfather of King David, as mentioned in Matthew 1:4–5. So Jesus' ancestor was a prostitute!

I find this amazing. God uses all sorts of people to bring about His plans and do great things. Noah, after his tremendous act of faith in building the ark, is found a few years later rolling around naked and drunk (Gen. 9:20–23); Jacob and Rebekah deceive Isaac to gain a blessing, by pretending that Jacob is his brother Esau (Gen. 27); David, considered to be Israel's greatest ever king, went on to commit adultery and have the woman's husband killed (2 Sam. 11).

So often we feel like we fail God and perhaps start to believe that because of this, He won't love us or use us for His purposes. But God delights in working through the most unlikely people. A quick read of Jesus' family tree will tell you that (see Matt. 1). So will looking around you at church on Sunday. God just loves people, warts and all.

PRAY

This kind of ironic humour gives us hope. We are just as undeserving of God's favour as the people we find in the Bible, but God's love and forgiveness are for us, just as they were for them. Thank God that He loves you as you are and wants to use you – despite your faults and failings.

KEY VERSE V8

'the sun blazed on Jonah's head so that he grew faint. He wanted to die, and said, "It would be better for me to die than to live."'

SATIRE IS THE use of humour to expose an unjust situation. It has a purpose. It uses the power of humour to change minds and influence events. It might be called the weapon of the weapon-less as it is often used by the underdog in a situation.

The book of Jonah is one of the best examples of satire in the Bible. Jonah finally makes it to Nineveh, moaning all the way, after initially being reluctant enough to run in the opposite direction. He then warns Nineveh of God's anger as he had been commanded to do, but when the people repent, God has mercy on them and Jonah finds another reason to sulk. In the passage we've just read, God makes His point to Jonah. The self-absorbed prophet is happy in the shade of the vine but when the vine withers, Jonah throws a huge strop (vv7–9).

God's point in verses 10–11 puts Jonah in his place. In all his self-absorbed sulking and moaning, Jonah had lost sight of the thousands of lost and helpless people who needed to hear God's message.

CHALLENGE

Although this satirical challenge is presented to Jonah, it is also a challenge for us. Are we tempted to care more about our own personal circumstances and wellbeing than about the millions of people in the world who don't know God?

READ:
MATTHEW 7:1–5

KEY VERSE V3

'Why do you look at the speck of sawdust in your brother's eye and pay no attention to the plank in your own eye?'

JESUS CERTAINLY WAS not a stand-up comedian. He did not use much 'laugh out loud funny' humour, but He often used irony, exaggeration and ridiculous or exaggerated pictures. You've probably heard of the horse with the 'long face' and the peanut that was 'assaulted'. And Jesus brings us the man trying to remove the speck of sawdust from his friend's eye when he has a huge plank of wood in his own. The visual humour is there, but we often miss it because we have read it so many times or because of the differences between our own culture and the culture of the time and place of Jesus on earth.

Imagine for a moment the image of this particular scenario: there's one man with a huge plank in his eye who is trying to remove the speck of sawdust from another man's eye. Through this ridiculous visual picture, Jesus is making a point. His use of humour adds colour and flavour to His message and helps us to remember it.

THINK
What do you use humour for? Do you just use it to amuse and entertain people, or even to put people down? Are there ways you could use humour to convey God's message?

KEY VERSE V24

'Again I tell you, it is easier for a camel to go through the eye of a needle than for someone who is rich to enter the kingdom of God.'

A MAN WHO has everything he could possibly desire comes to Jesus and wants a guarantee that he will get to heaven. Jesus tells him to give all his wealth away to the poor and follow Him, but the man goes away sad. For this man, his money and possessions were the stumbling block to following Jesus, and Jesus again uses a ridiculous, exaggerated image to make His point. The idea of a camel trying to squeeze itself through the eye of a needle illustrates just how hard it is for this man to enter the kingdom of God.

Some commentaries say that 'The Eye of the Needle' was a gate in Jerusalem which was so low that a camel could only pass through it if the camel had all its baggage removed and crawled on its knees. However there is no evidence or architectural record for such a gate, so I think the illustration stands as the ridiculously comical one that it is. The challenge remains then: what do you need to give up in order to live Jesus' way more fully? What is making it as hard for you to follow Jesus as it is for a camel to squeeze through the eye of a needle?

PRAY

Is there something you are reluctant to give up that is not God's ideal for you? Perhaps an unhelpful influence in your life or an unhealthy habit? Pray that God will help you let go of it and draw you into a closer relationship with Him.

READ:
MATTHEW 23:13–36

KEY VERSE v27

'you hypocrites! You are like whitewashed tombs, which look beautiful on the outside but on the inside are full of the bones of the dead and everything unclean.'

THIS PASSAGE MIGHT be shocking to those who still believe in a 'meek and mild' Jesus. He certainly gives the Pharisees a dressing-down here. The Pharisees were the religious leaders; the equivalent of your vicar or your youth worker, but they were preaching one thing and living another. This is a good example of Jesus using satire to make a point. It may be a harsh criticism to say that they looked great on the outside but inside were rotten and full of death and decay, like a clean, white-washed tomb. Yet the Pharisees' words and lifestyle did not measure up and Jesus has no time for hypocrites.

I once had to have a hard conversation with a volunteer youth worker I knew. When challenged on his lifestyle issues of regularly getting drunk and sleeping with strangers, he responded, 'What does it matter as long as nobody else knows?' It is really important in our Christian life to live with integrity. If you attend church on Sunday and youth group midweek, do and say all the right things, pray with enthusiasm or even lead the worship band, but would not want the church to know about your less public habits, perhaps Jesus' words to the Pharisees might be a challenge to you.

PRAY
Commit your words and lifestyle to God. Ask Him to help you live with integrity and to highlight any of your habits that need to change to make this possible.

KEY VERSE V27

"'First let the children eat all they want," he told her, "for it is not right to take the children's bread and toss it to the dogs.'"

THIS PASSAGE IS puzzling but clearly shows Jesus' wit. A woman comes to Jesus and begs Him to heal her daughter. Jesus then seems to say that He cannot heal her daughter because she is a dog. Taken at its face value, the sentence is rude and insulting. How can we possibly accept such a picture of Christ? The woman responds, however, with even sharper wit, that even dogs can eat the crumbs that fall from the table. Jesus then immediately tells her that He has healed her daughter. This is a strange account indeed. The theologian Trueblood unpacks it and argues that, 'The clue to Christ's spirit in the entire encounter is His immediate affirmation and friendly response to the woman's wit.'[1] Jesus' remarks were an example of humorous banter. Sharp, witty humour is exchanged here but through it, serious issues are addressed, and Jesus responds with a miracle.

Humour is a way to express serious things. Laughter relaxes people. The jokes can raise issues that may not be raised anywhere else and if it can be joked about, it can be talked about.

CHALLENGE

So often, we can drift through life on a fairly superficial level. When did you last talk to your closest friend about the deeper issues of life? What struggles is he or she going through? Do what you can to start a meaningful conversation.

---

[1] E. Trueblood, *The Humour of Christ* (San Francisco: Harper, 1990) p122

WEEKEND
26/27 NOV

READ:
LUKE 15:1–7

KEY VERSES 1–2

'Now the tax collectors and sinners were all gathering round to hear Jesus. But the Pharisees and the teachers of the law muttered, "This man welcomes sinners, and eats with them."'

ONE OF THE greatest positive uses of humour is the way it can be used to break a tense situation. Wyndham Lewis once said that, 'Laughter is the mind sneezing.'[1]

Comedian Andy Kind jokes about an awkward situation on a train when he and his friend were on the way back from a football match. The fans of the opposing team boarded the train and there was soon tension and a face-to-face stand-off. Andy was wearing his team's shirt, Stoke City, whose football strip is red and white stripes.

▼

▼

▼

▼

▼

▼

At just the right moment in the midst of this tense situation a small child in the carriage pointed to Andy and piped up with the words, 'I've found Wally.'

The tension was broken, laughter ensued and a fight was averted through the insight and humour of this child.

This story highlights the positive use of humour to avoid a conflict situation. This is exactly what Jesus does in the passage from Luke. The Pharisees and teachers of the law were itching for a fight and full of criticism that Jesus was mixing with sinners. Instead of grappling with them and causing further conflict, Jesus told stories and humorous ones at that! Who in their right mind would really leave their ninety-nine sheep to go and hunt for the missing one? Jesus would, but at first glance it seems ridiculous.

Sometimes the wisest thing to do in a tense situation is to avoid the conflict while it is heated. It should perhaps be addressed later, but after the tension has eased. Sometimes the best thing is to lighten the situation, maybe with a well-placed joke or a story.

CHALLENGE

Next time you disagree with someone, try not to rise to the temptation of fuelling the argument. Instead, take a breath and lighten the situation. Come back to it later, when the heat has gone out of the moment.

[1] Tal Bonham, *Humour: God's Gift* (Tennessee: Broadman Press, 1988) p18

READ:
MARK 10:35–45

KEY VERSE v45

'For even the Son of Man did not come to be served, but to serve, and to give his life as a ransom for many.'

A LOT OF jokes are about incongruity – to do with broken rules and surprising meanings. The build-up of a joke leads you to expect a certain outcome, and then the punchline overturns your expectations. Jesus Himself was an incongruity. In everything He did, He overturned expectations. People expected a king on a powerful horse, and He arrived in Jerusalem on a donkey. People expected a warrior and He came to bring peace. People expected a ruler and Jesus came as a servant.

In a world that says we need to make money and own a nice car and a big house to be successful, Jesus calls us to follow His example and live lives of incongruity. In a world where it's apparently acceptable to put others down to make ourselves look better and climb over others to get up the career ladder, we are called to live humbly and to serve others. In a world that encourages us to get as much as we can, Jesus urges us to give. The challenge for us is to be the punchline and be the opposite of the egocentric world around us; to be servant-hearted, generous, humble, and to love our enemies.

THINK

'So the last will be first, and the first will be last' (Matt. 20:16). Reflect on those words. How might they affect your attitudes and lifestyle?

KEY VERSE V24

'But God raised him from the dead, freeing him from the agony of death, because it was impossible for death to keep its hold on him.'

OF COURSE, THE greatest incongruity of Jesus' life is in death; in the cross and resurrection. People's expectations were that death was the end, but Jesus turned it all on its head. He turned the whole of history upside down by coming back to life! Death could not keep Him in its grip. In some traditions, Christians celebrate Holy Humour Sunday[1] at Easter, celebrating the huge joke that God pulled on Satan by bringing Jesus back to life from death.

As Christians, we are 'Easter people' rejoicing in life after death. We should not dwell on the darkness and suffering of the cross without rejoicing in the new life available to us. When we approach spring, we see signs of new life appearing. Trees and plants that seemed dead not long ago begin to blossom. The whole of creation recognises and echoes Jesus' resurrection and the new life He offers us.

PRAY

Thank God for Jesus' resurrection and the new life available to us because of it. Death has been overcome. Jesus has opened up the way for us to enter the kingdom of heaven. Pray that we might live with our future hope in mind.

[1] Sometimes called 'Laetare Sunday'. See http://en.wikipedia.org/wiki/Laetare_Sunday to find out more

READ:
LAMENTATIONS 3:1–24

KEY VERSE v14

'I became the laughing-stock of all my people; they mock me in song all day long.'

WHEN YOU ARE having a hard time, just have a read of this passage. Lamentations is a true piece of lamenting and raw, open pain. The author is incredibly honest with God in a way that may shock us, and yet he still seems to hang on to hope in God, even if by the skin of his teeth. In verses 22–24, he remembers that even in his suffering, 'The faithful love of the LORD never ends! His mercies never cease' (NLT). Lamentations, Job and the Psalms show us that we too can be as honest with God about our struggles and the things that upset us. If we want to shout at God for something, that is OK. He is big enough to cope.

In verse 14 though, the author laments his so-called friends laughing at him and even making up and singing mocking songs about him. Some friends, eh? He is at his lowest point and even his friends let him down.

Have you ever laughed at the expense of someone else, or kicked them while they were down? Perhaps you have been the butt of jokes yourself or have had people talk about you in a negative way. Gossip is always destructive. Why not try some good gossiping instead? Say nice things about people behind their backs. It's a great feeling and can really build people up.

THINK
How often is your humour about putting other people down? Do you need to make any changes in this area?

READ:
EPHESIANS 5:1–20

KEY VERSE V4

'Nor should there be obscenity, foolish talk or coarse joking, which are out of place, but rather thanksgiving.'

THURS 1 DEC

IT'S FAR TOO easy to join in when other people are gossiping or bad-mouthing someone behind their backs. And even if we don't join in, it's almost as bad to stay silent and not challenge conversations that ridicule people and belittle them. A rude, racist, sexist or homophobic joke might make us feel part of the crowd if we laugh, or look a bit edgy if we repeat it, but Paul is very clear that this kind of behaviour is not for us. Writing to the Ephesians, he spells out that this kind of humour is not fitting for us as Christians.

As we have already seen, humour is often about opposites. Paul encourages us to think and talk in an 'opposite' manner. Instead of sharing crude jokes and off-colour comments, he encourages us to 'let there be thankfulness to God' (NLT). Let's make sure our words and actions are life-affirming, positive, generous and kind.

THINK

Do you worry about what other people will think of you if you do not laugh at or participate in humour that is 'coarse' and offensive? What impact might it have on others if you are brave enough to stand up against negative humour?

READ:
PHILIPPIANS 4:1–9

KEY VERSE V8

'whatever is true, whatever is noble,
whatever is right, whatever is pure,
whatever is lovely, whatever is admirable
– if anything is excellent or praiseworthy
– think about such things.'

I'M NOT SURE what I can say to add to this passage. Coming to the end of our series on humour we have explored different types and different uses of humour. Many are useful tools for making a point or making things better. Others are negative and need to be kept in check.

This passage from Philippians is generally a good rule of thumb for how we use humour, but likewise a good guideline for life generally as a Christian. You might like to use it as a mantra when you get out of bed and start the day. It is a good target to aim for in your thoughts.

Revisiting one of our earlier Bible studies, laughter is good for us and is part of what it means to be human. It's obvious that as God created us, He created us with the capacity to laugh and have fun. As we end this series on humour, let's reflect on this quote from Mike Riddell: 'When there are tears of laughter alongside the ritual and prayer and singing, then we know that Jesus is once more in the world.'[1]

CHALLENGE
Honour God with everything you are, including your sense of humour.

[1] Mike Riddell, *Threshold of the Future: Reforming the Church in the Post-Christian West (Gospel and Cultures)* (London: SPCK Publishing, 1999) p127

READ:
EPHESIANS 5:15–33

KEY VERSE
V21

'Submit to one another out of reverence for Christ.'

PT2
OBEDIENCE

IN PART ONE, we unpacked what it means to obey God. We now move on to discuss obeying other people. It's important to know who to obey. When I was little, my mum told me not to play with the electric fire in our living room. If I hadn't obeyed her, I could have ended up with some nasty burns. On the other hand, some people will try to influence you to drink too much, take drugs or steal from shops. If you blindly obey them, you can end up in a real mess. So who should we obey, and why?

CONTINUED▶

CONTINUED▶▶

Over the next couple of weeks we'll discuss what obedience looks like. We'll also look at what we should do if obeying another person would compromise our obedience to God.

The first good reason for obeying other people is that this is an important part of obeying God. In today's reading, Paul urges us that submitting to God should lead us to submit to one another. We should be humble enough to put other people first, rather than insisting on getting our own way. Submitting to people can feel uncomfortable, just as submitting to God can. But Paul is not insisting that we behave like a doormat for anyone who wants to take advantage of us. The key is that submission and love go hand in hand. God's ideal is that we should submit to each other and love the people who have submitted to us. Submitting to someone makes us vulnerable, but we can feel secure in this if we know that the person loves us.

So, whatever happens, let's serve people around us, but if they show us no love or respect we don't have to let them walk all over us. In turn, think about who's serving you. Are you showing them love?

THINK

How willing are you to submit to people? Do you need to make any changes to how you show your obedience to God through others?

KEY VERSE V17

'Have confidence in your leaders and submit to their authority'

I WAS RECENTLY in a fairly dull meeting at church. We were discussing routine and unexciting things, but the meeting suddenly got livelier when someone questioned a decision the vicar had made. If this guy had been satisfied with simply questioning the decision it wouldn't have been remarkable, but he went on to tear into the vicar, lambasting him for acting without the committee's approval. It seemed that the guy was happy for the vicar to lead the church and make decisions until he actually led the church and made decisions!

We might not always feel like obeying our spiritual leaders. They might make unpopular decisions or ask us to do things we don't feel like doing, but leadership means making decisions, and decisions don't always make a leader popular. It's OK to ask our church leaders and youth leaders questions when we don't understand what they're doing, but let's always be respectful, honouring and biblical in the way we question them, and in our response to their answers. And it's always fine to examine things they say and check that they line up with Scripture.

PRAY

Ask for God's blessing on your church leaders. Ask that He will give them wisdom in their decisions and help the whole church, including you, to submit to their leadership when it's in line with God's leadership.

READ:
EPHESIANS 6:5-9

KEY VERSE V5

'Slaves, obey your earthly masters with respect and fear, and with sincerity of heart, just as you would obey Christ.'

HOW DO YOU treat your teachers – or your boss? I've known teachers and bosses who were easy to respect, as well as others who seemed to me to be a bit annoying or ridiculous. In particular, I can think of teachers who were completely clueless and who were tormented by my friends and me. We were out of order, of course. Nobody deserves to be treated like that.

The challenge for us is to show 'deep respect' for anyone in authority over us, whether we think they deserve it or not. Obeying God should be reflected in the way we treat people, and the respect we show to our bosses and teachers is a very powerful way for our lifestyle to reflect God's truth. Perhaps it would help to imagine Jesus with you as you stack the shelves, deliver the papers or do your course work. What would He have to say about your attitude? We might not be slaves these days, but it is still important that we respect and honour people in authority over us.

CHALLENGE

I'm sure you can think of at least one person in authority over you whom you struggle to respect. When you next see or speak to them, choose to speak and act in a way that respects this person.

'Honour your father and your mother, as the LORD your God has commanded you'

I KNOW THIS isn't going to make me popular, but it really is important to respect our parents. (Please resist the temptation to throw things at me!) Honouring (and obeying) our parents won't always be easy. There will probably be times when we feel misunderstood or unfairly treated. And, of course, we can express our opinions but, even when we disagree with our parents, we should still respect them and their point of view.

Occasionally, we are justified in disagreeing with our parents and doing what we think is right, but unless there are extreme circumstances these occasions should be rare. Our habit should be to obey them. And when we do disagree with mum and dad, let's do so in a way which still honours and respects them.

The commandment to honour our parents comes with a promise: this will bring a blessing to us (Deut. 5:16; Exod. 20:12). God doesn't tell us to obey our parents just to give us more rules to follow; He knows that this way genuinely is best for us.

THINK
When are you most tempted not to obey your parents? Are you ever justified in this? How can you handle disagreements with your parents positively?

🗇 **KEY VERSE** V7

'"Do all that you have in mind," his armour-bearer said. "Go ahead; I am with you heart and soul."'

RALLY DRIVERS CAN seem pretty reckless: they swing their cars along narrow, winding roads, with seemingly no thought for the potential of instant death if they misjudge a corner. But the real hero is the co-driver; the person who sits in the passenger seat, ignores the lethal danger they face and calmly gives the driver instructions for the next turn. The co-driver has to trust the driver completely. One false move from the driver and they both could end up in hospital -- or worse. But the co-driver still does their job and shows unwavering loyalty to their driver.

Respect and obedience are strongly linked to loyalty. Jonathan's idea to attack a Philistine outpost probably seemed crazy, but the armour-bearer stuck with him. He chose to trust Jonathan, stay loyal to him and obey him. The result was an incredible victory. How willing are you to stick with someone in a difficult situation? If you only obey someone when it's easy, that's not real obedience. If you trust someone fully, and a relationship has grown and developed based on mutual trust and respect, then staying loyal when life gets hard is much easier to do. Amazing things can happen if we're willing to do that.

THINK
Who do you trust? How far would your loyalty to this person stretch? Pray that God would give you courage and stickability when life gets tough.

KEY VERSE V6

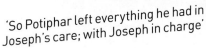

'So Potiphar left everything he had in Joseph's care; with Joseph in charge'

RESPECT, LOYALTY AND obedience require you to act with integrity – even when no one is looking! Don't be surprised when your obedience to someone prompts them to give you big opportunities and big responsibilities. Of course, you may also face the temptation to abuse the position you're in.

Joseph's obedience to Potiphar led to responsibility for everything Potiphar owned. It also led to an opportunity to sleep with Potiphar's wife. Quite possibly, he could have done it and got away with it. But Joseph had too much integrity for that. He knew that Potiphar trusted him completely and that obeying Potiphar meant honouring the trust his boss had shown him. For Joseph, obedience meant respecting Potiphar when his back was turned, not just when he was watching.

What tempts us might be different from what tempted Joseph, but the challenge for us is the same: true obedience – godly obedience – means respecting someone, whether they're watching you or not.

CHALLENGE

How much respect do you show people when their backs are turned? Do you find yourself grumbling, gossiping and taking advantage of them? Do you need to make any changes here?

WEEKEND
10/11 DEC

READ:
DANIEL 2:1–19

KEY VERSE v19

'During the night the mystery was revealed to Daniel in a vision. Then Daniel praised the God of heaven'

BILLY GRAHAM IS best known as an evangelist and Christian leader, but he has also spent time with no fewer than 12 presidents of the United States. He was a particularly close adviser to Richard Nixon, regularly leading private church services at the White House during Nixon's presidency, and offering him guidance at the height of the Watergate scandal. Billy has had a huge influence on some of the most powerful men in the world, and was hailed by one former president as 'America's pastor'. Billy's obedience to God and his faithful serving of people in power presented him with a position of real influence. Billy used this position to bring God's wisdom into hard and vitally important situations. This did not always mean agreeing with the presidents he served, but it did always mean respecting them and speaking God's truth.

Daniel's experience was similar. Simply through doing his best to serve God and serve the king, he found himself in a position of influence he would never have expected. Billy and Daniel both found that if we're willing to obey God, and loyally and respectfully serve the people in authority over us, we may get some surprising opportunities to share God's truth with powerful people. We won't all have the chance to advise world leaders, as Daniel and Billy Graham did. But obedience to God can make us more open to His wisdom, which often means that we receive insights other people won't have thought of. Showing respect and a servant attitude to powerful people can give us opportunities to share these insights with them.

PRAY

Lord God, thank You for being the source of all wisdom. As I try to obey You and serve people in authority, please help me to share Your wisdom with them. Amen.

READ:
ROMANS 13:1-7

KEY VERSE V1

'Let everyone be subject to the governing authorities, for there is no authority except that which God has established.'

OBEYING PEOPLE IN authority over us includes obeying the government. Hmmm. Does that mean we should never object or protest or hold the government accountable for what they do? I don't think so. We'll think about this a little more over the next few days but in the meantime, let's remember that our usual response should be to submit to our government.

Paul, writing in Romans, tells us that our leaders are in power because God put them there. Before you start mentioning Hitler, Stalin and Mugabe, these guys are very extreme examples of bad leadership. The majority of national leaders do a great job, work tirelessly and have their people's best interests at heart. So our default setting should be to obey them. Of course there are exceptions. Of course there will be times when we disagree with our leaders. But, more often than not, our responsibility is to obey, keep to the law and, yes, pay our taxes!

CHALLENGE

God wants us to submit to our government. This means keeping to the law. Are you compromising on this at all - perhaps you download music illegally? Resolve to stick to the whole law, not just the bits you like. The only exception to this is when the law requires you to compromise your faith, and this is a very rare thing.

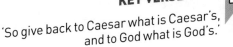

KEY VERSE V21

'So give back to Caesar what is Caesar's,
and to God what is God's.'

I OWE DIFFERENT things to different people. I owe my bank about £2,000 for a loan they gave me to buy a car. I owe my boss about 38 hours' work per week. I owe my friends a few favours for all the times they've helped me decorate my house, jump-started my car and babysat for my son. But what do I owe the government?

This was what the Pharisees' disciples asked Jesus. They were trying to trap Jesus into either breaking the Roman law or upsetting the Jewish crowd. Jesus' answer is wonderful. He makes it clear that it is possible to obey our government while also obeying God. However, He also makes it clear that there are limits to the government's authority over us. For the Romans, the emperor was a god. Full obedience to him meant not just loyalty and paying taxes; it meant worshipping him.

Jesus' point is that a government deserves what belongs to them, but so does God. Our government have a right to ask for taxes, but only God can ask for our souls. We should obey our government, but our ultimate obedience and ultimate loyalty should be God's and God's alone.

PRAY
Commit yourself to obey God above anyone else. Ask for His wisdom in how far your obedience to other people should go.

READ:
PROVERBS 16:10–16

KEY VERSE v13

'Kings take pleasure in honest lips; they value the one who speaks what is right.'

KINGS VALUE HONESTY. So let's speak up when there's something wrong. A leader needs wise, humble but godly, advice. We can influence our leaders in this way. If you see something that goes against God's will, speak up. Obeying our Government doesn't mean just going with the flow.

In ancient Israel, the prophet and the king worked in partnership. The king's role was to lead; the prophet's role was to advise him and bring God's perspective to his decisions. That sometimes meant being outspoken or bringing a message that was hard for the king to hear. For example, Nathan encouraged David that God's blessing would always be on his family (2 Sam. 7), but later challenged and rebuked him, after David had committed adultery (2 Sam. 12). Good kings valued the prophets' perspective, even if it wasn't what they wanted to hear. Later prophets, though, brought such strident challenges to their kings that they ended up imprisoned, beaten or even killed.

We can have a prophetic role too, speaking God's truth to our leaders, respectfully protesting if God's will seems to be compromised. Fortunately, for many of us, we're unlikely to end up in prison for doing this!

THINK
What might God say about what your leaders are doing? Pray about this and don't be afraid to encourage or challenge them as appropriate.

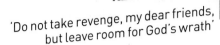

KEY VERSE V19

'Do not take revenge, my dear friends,
but leave room for God's wrath'

SOMEONE JOSTLES YOU in a school corridor, so you push them back. They push you harder, so you hit them. Then they hit you. And so it continues. Before you know it, it's an all-out fight. Or maybe a friend makes a careless comment about you. You get upset and say something worse about them. Then they get angry and give you a mouthful of abuse. You give a mouthful back. An icy silence follows and you start avoiding each other. In either case, our instinct to take revenge makes the conflict worse.

Perhaps God insists that only He should take revenge because only He really knows what someone who hurt us was thinking, and only He can be trusted to judge people completely fairly. If someone in authority makes life hard for us, we still shouldn't take revenge, even if they seem to be going against God. We can speak up, we can protest, but if we aim to take revenge it does our cause and God's cause no good at all. The American Civil Rights Movement in the 1950s and 1960s was renowned for protesting about racial inequality powerfully, but peacefully and prayerfully. If we're treated unfairly, we can do the same, but only God should take revenge on the people who persecute us.

 PRAY

Pray for the people who make your life difficult. Even if you sometimes feel you would like to see them suffer, ask God to bless them and help you through the difficulty.

READ:
ACTS 4:1–22

KEY VERSE v20

'As for us, we cannot help speaking about what we have seen and heard.'

NOT TOO LONG ago, more than 3,000 Christians were driven from their homes in Ethiopia when Muslim extremists set fire to churches and houses. In the same month, a man from Bangladesh was sentenced to a year in prison for selling Christian books, and two Christian men were killed outside a church in Pakistan. This is real persecution.

Peter and John's circumstances were just as extreme. They know that they could be imprisoned or worse for following Jesus. (In fact, of Jesus' 12 original disciples, all but Judas later faced severe persecution and almost all were executed for their faith.) And yet, Peter and John respond to this danger with courage and determination. They are resolved to speak out for God, whatever the opposition, and they tell the ruling council exactly that!

In comparison to the persecution that the first disciples suffered (and which our Christian brothers and sisters around the world still suffer), we have it easy. Yes, we might encounter opposition because of what we believe, but nowhere near this extreme. So let's speak God's truth boldly! And if anyone challenges us, let's tell them clearly that we will obey God, not them.

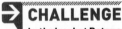

CHALLENGE
Let's do what Peter and John did and tell the people around us what God has done for us. If that seems intimidating, let's pray for courage, strength and protection.

KEY VERSE
V5

'he saved us, not because of righteous things we had done, but because of his mercy.'

PT3
DISCIPLE-SHIP

TIME FOR THE final instalment in our series on discipleship. Let's kick off with a few verses from Titus. Paul is writing to Titus, who is in Crete at the time, to encourage him to continue working with these guys even though it was hard and they were messing him around. Paul gives Titus some practical tips about how he could help the Cretans to overcome their past way of life and launch out into living brand-new Christian lives.

CONTINUED▸▸

Have you ever made a mistake? Ever done some really good things for others? Well, God loves you no matter how many mistakes you've made or how many good deeds you've done – or any combination of the two. God's love isn't something we have to work really hard to earn – it's a free gift! And because of God's love, He has saved us from the mess of our old life and set us up clean and ready for our new life. God has dealt with our past, so we don't have to let it hold us back. We're free to live God's way!

DISCIPLESHIP TIP 22:

Remember that God loves you and has saved you, no matter how many good or bad things you've done. He loves us – not because we deserve it, but just because He's so good!

THINK

Over the next few days we will be looking at living as a disciple through Jesus: how this works and what it means to us today.

God washed away our sins, giving us a new birth and new life through the Holy Spirit. He generously poured out the Spirit upon us because of what Jesus did. He declared us not guilty because of His great kindness. And now we know that we will inherit eternal life.

IN HIS LETTER to the Colossian Christians, Paul outlines how we should live as disciples because of the new life God has given us. He explains how we should interact with others and respond to situations around us.

We all have faults and it's probably easier to see them in other people than in ourselves. But just think how long it took you to learn to ride a bike, drive a car or speak another language. It took time, it took patience and it took others investing in you. It's just the same in working out your new life: it takes time to change and, believe it or not, others might need to forgive you – possibly because of something you said or did.

As a member of a youth group, I used to pick on one particular guy. When I started to take my new life seriously, I wanted to stop and say sorry. He very graciously accepted my apology, but he could easily have told me to get lost.

DISCIPLESHIP TIP 23:
Learn to forgive others and to say sorry to others for your mistakes. Make time to do it – you will benefit from it.

THINK

Do you need to take your life as a disciple seriously? Do you need to start living it – and making your actions match your words? Do you need to say sorry?

Do you need to forgive someone – even if they haven't said sorry to you? Talk to God and forgive them. Allow God to do the rest.

READ:
2 CORINTHIANS 5:14–21

KEY VERSE V20

'We are therefore Christ's ambassadors, as though God were making his appeal through us. We implore you on Christ's behalf: be reconciled to God.'

I ONCE HAD to attend a dinner reception as a representative of an organisation; we were all there in our dinner jackets or evening dresses. Each of us was aware that we had to circulate and chat to as many people as possible, telling them about our organisation and pretending to listen and be really interested when they told us about theirs.

We were all ambassadors of our organisations but, to be honest, the evening seemed to many of us to be a bit false. We were all dressed up, on our best behaviour and making efforts to be nice.

Life is not like this. We get up late, we spill cereal down our shirts, we have bad hair days – and we are not always nice! But, as disciples of Christ, we are God's mouthpiece to the world – to those who know Him and those who don't – every day.

DISCIPLESHIP TIP 24:

Every morning, get up and say: 'I am an ambassador of Christ.' And be confident that He is with you, helping you when you speak.

CHALLENGE

It takes effort to remember that God wants to use us every day to tell others about Him. Not in a false way, but in a living way: the way in which we live our lives.

'not giving up meeting together, as some are in the habit of doing, but encouraging one another'

WED 21 DEC

HOW OFTEN DO you get together with other Christian friends? Is it just at church on a Sunday or a mid-week group? Do you meet up apart from at organised events?

Jesus taught His disciples to meet together, to share meals together and to lovingly question each other. It is the same with us now. Jesus loves us to meet up with other Christians. Although He has called us to tell those who don't know Him about our lives with Him, He also loves it when we meet together with other Christians.

This 'fellowship' is an important part of our lives with Jesus. It's really helpful to hang out with others who have the same joys and trials of being a Christian. Now that Christmas is only just around the corner, why don't you arrange to meet up with some friends just to have fun. Remember to invite God to be with you.

DISCIPLESHIP TIP 25:

Christmas is a great time to tell others about Jesus so when you next meet up with your Christian mates, why not take a non-Christian friend with you? Be yourself and they will soon see that being a Christian isn't weird!

PRAY

Father, thank You for my Christian friends. Please help me to support and encourage them. Challenge me to invite all my friends to mix together and to remember to invite You into those times too. Amen.

READ:
GALATIANS 5:22–26

KEY VERSE V25

'Since we live by the Spirit, let us keep in step with the Spirit.'

I AM SURE that by now you are surrounded by Christmas trees! But how do you tell what type of tree you are looking at? One way is by the fruit it produces – an apple tree does not produce bananas. And this is exactly the same in our lives: how we speak and act is a reflection of what we are really like; what kind of a person we are. If we're rooted in God, we produce good fruit. God sent a Helper and Encourager to develop this kind of fruit in us.

Have you ever had anyone show you kindness? My car broke down once on the middle of a roundabout. Traffic was building up and people were beeping their horns. I got out and tried to push the car to one side – quite a task when you are by yourself. Someone got out of his car, helped me and gave me a lift home. That was ten years ago now and I still remember his kindness.

As a disciple of Christ, are you living every day letting the Holy Spirit lead you? Do your words and actions show this?

DISCIPLESHIP TIP 26:

Remember this – 'But the Holy Spirit produces this kind of fruit in our lives: love, joy, peace, patience, kindness, goodness, faithfulness, gentleness, and self-control' (Gal. 5:22–23, NLT).

CHALLENGE

What will you be remembered for? What fruit do you show? Are you allowing the Holy Spirit to do His work in your life?

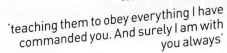

KEY VERSE V20

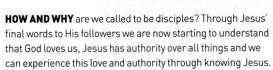

'teaching them to obey everything I have commanded you. And surely I am with you always'

HOW AND WHY are we called to be disciples? Through Jesus' final words to His followers we are now starting to understand that God loves us, Jesus has authority over all things and we can experience this love and authority through knowing Jesus.

In today's reading, we find Jesus about to go back to heaven. The disciples are probably worried and uncertain about what will happen next. But Jesus knows every detail: the Holy Spirit will come and thousands of people will start to follow Him. He knows how each of the disciples will react to this and the roles they will play. And He reassures them: 'I am with you always.'

Jesus also knows how you are going to react to situations in your life and He reassures you: 'I am with you always.' Wherever you are today, Jesus is with you and wants to be involved. This could either be really scary: 'Jesus is watching!' Or really comforting: 'Jesus is with you.' Subtle difference! Jesus is not like a spectator judging how you are doing, but a friend who knows you and wants to help you.

DISCIPLESHIP TIP 27:
Jesus is there to help – remember to ask Him.

PRAY
Father, please help me to understand that You want to be involved in my life – not to tell me where I'm going wrong but to show me where I can go right. Thank You for always being there for me. Amen.

WEEKEND
24/25 DEC

READ:
JOHN 17:11–15

KEY VERSE VV11–12

'Holy Father, protect them by the power of your name ... While I was with them, I protected them and kept them safe'

IT IS GREAT to be with friends and family at Christmas time. As you celebrate Christmas this weekend, think about whether you have ever had to leave some good friends behind. How did that feel? When I moved away to go to university I had to leave some really close friends at home. I was sure we'd stay in touch but I still knew I'd miss them a lot. While I was away it was hard when I knew my friends at home were struggling, but it was a comfort to know that God was with them when I couldn't be and that He was looking after them.

When Jesus knew He was about to leave His disciples – His closest friends – it must have been incredibly hard for Him. As He prays, He asks God to look after the disciples, to keep them and care for them. He passes on His love, because He is going to be with God the Father. Jesus can no longer be around in human form to care for the disciples and so He prays that His Father will protect them. The Holy Spirit will be sent later to fill, help and strengthen the disciples.

For us today, never having experienced being directly looked after by Jesus' human hand, it might seem a bit confusing; but Jesus and God the Father were arranging things the way we know them today. The Father keeps us and cares for us; Jesus is in the middle, talking to the Father on our behalf; and the Holy Spirit helps us to live God's way. We are under God's protection in the world and protected by His name until we come home to Him – when we will be with Him for eternity.

DISCIPLESHIP TIP 28:
Jesus is with us and has asked for Father God's protection over our lives. That's so comforting! Live every day in this knowledge.

THINK
This Christmas, think about what knowing God means to you. Is there anyone in particular who you think may need God's love this weekend? As well as praying for that person, maybe you could share the knowledge from Discipleship Tip 28 with them? Happy Christmas!

READ:
JOHN 17:16–20

KEY VERSE v20
'My prayer is not for them alone. I pray also for those who will believe in me through their message'

WHAT DOES TODAY'S key verse mean for each one of us? We have to tell other people about God. In Jesus' 'Great Commission' we are told to 'go and make disciples of all nations, baptising them in the name of the Father and of the Son and of the Holy Spirit' (see Matt. 28:18–20). Think about it. One of the reasons we know about Jesus is because of others telling us about Him; through their testimony, their story of how they met Him. Here Jesus is praying for all the people who are going to believe in Him because of what these disciples say.

This means two things: One – Jesus is praying directly for you, just as He was 2,000 years ago. Two – He is praying for all those people you talk to and who come to know Him because of your story.

DISCIPLESHIP TIP 29:
Go and tell others about Jesus! Be assured and encouraged that Jesus is talking to God about you and them.

CHALLENGE
Could you explain why you became a Christian in a simple way? Remember that Jesus is praying for those who come to know Him through your story. This implies that He is expecting you to share that story with others!

KEY VERSE V27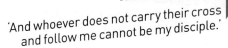

'And whoever does not carry their cross and follow me cannot be my disciple.'

SOON THE JANUARY sales will be in full swing, but if money were no object, what would be the first thing you'd run out and buy? A nice new phone? A year's supply of top quality chocolate? A Greek island? In our heads we all have dreams in which money stops being a barrier and everything becomes possible. The reality is that good things have a cost attached to them, and great things have a greater cost to them.

A relationship with Jesus is a free one, but a costly one. Free, because grace doesn't have to be earned for our sins to be forgiven, and having our relationship with God restored is offered to us freely. However, being a disciple involves us giving things up in life. Being a Christian could cost us status, money, or even some relationships. But the rewards are always worth the cost.

In this passage Jesus does something both shocking and surprisingly common. He turns to a large gathering of followers and challenges them. He needs to challenge them because many have got caught up in all the miracles, the free lunches and the overall hype, but they need to know that there is a real cost to following God, and it's a cost that many people turn away from. Will you count up the cost and dive in?

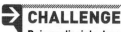

CHALLENGE
Being a disciple does have a real cost to it. Have you weighed up the cost?

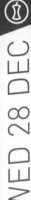

READ:
MATTHEW 4:18–22

 KEY VERSES vv21b–22

'Jesus called them, and immediately they left the boat and their father and followed him.'

WHAT WOULD IT take for you to drop everything right now? To just leave behind everything you hold important in life. Imagine your favourite celebrity coming into your room right now and asking whether they could come and hang out with you for a while – you'd probably say yes, right? What if that celebrity then told you that hanging out might have a bit of a cost attached? That you weren't going to be able to go on social media for a while, that you won't have home-comforts, that your life might start to look very different from how it looked before. Would you still say yes?

Being a disciple has a cost. It had a cost for the guys in this Bible passage – they had to leave the life they were so comfortable with and follow Jesus into the unknown. But they chose Him over their comfort. Are we prepared to weigh up the cost of being a disciple, knowing that our lives may never be the same as a result? Are we prepared to give up our known comforts for an unknown adventure with Jesus?

THINK

If Jesus told you to leave your life as you know it right now in order to follow Him, would you say yes?

KEY VERSE V32

'Then you will know the truth, and the truth will set you free.'

MANY PEOPLE ARE searching for truth. They think they know where it is but can't quite locate it. People look to religions, consumerism, relationships and even the internet to find answers to life's questions.

Most worldviews, religions and even secular views point somewhere else for the truth to be found. This could be Mohammed pointing to Allah, Buddhism pointing to the self or Atheism pointing towards science or self-gratification. Jesus is the only character in history bold enough to point to Himself as being the truth. With Jesus, the search is over, the reason for living is found. The massive questions of life are answered with the truth. Choosing to believe that Jesus is the truth is what we call faith, and it's one of the most important parts of being a disciple.

DISCIPLESHIP TIP 30:

Remember that discipleship is more about faith than feelings. Faith is choosing to believe what's true, and we can choose to believe that Jesus is the way, the truth and the life even if we're not feeling a spiritual high.

PRAY

Lord God, thank You that in You we have truth, that the answers to life's questions can be found in Jesus. Help us to have faith in You, by choosing to believe what is really true. Amen.

READ:
JOHN 16:12–15

 KEY VERSE v13

'But when he, the Spirit of truth, comes, he will guide you into all the truth.'

JESUS, IN HIS time on earth, taught us a lot about what it means to be a disciple and we've studied many of these things over the last few months. Reading the Bible and thinking about His wise words are really important. But it's also really important to know that we have a guide with us who can lead us in the ways of discipleship.

Listening to the Holy Spirit is one of the key disciplines of being a disciple, because it's learning to be in tune with God's presence on earth.

We are often so busy that we don't give time to listen to the voice of God. We are so keen with the results of being a disciple but not keen to do the whole process, because we know that sometimes keeping in tune with the Spirit can be time consuming and tough. Making time to listen and be guided by God can be the last thing we want to do with our days when TV, social networks, friends and games consoles beckon us. However, discipline comes from the word disciple.

DISCIPLESHIP TIP 31:
If you want to be a true follower of Jesus, you need to listen and plug into the Holy Spirit, even when it seems tough to do so.

 THINK
Are you giving the Holy Spirit enough time and space to guide you today?